MEDITERRANEN DIET

100 Fast, Healthy And Delicious Recipes

Mussels with Potatoes and Olives 31
Cicoria e Fagiolo 33
Savory Pancake with Lemon-Dill Yogurt 34
Chicken and Spinach Wrap 35
Broccoli Rabe with Cherry Peppers 36
Beet, Chickpea and Almond Dip with Pita Chips 37
Mediterranean Greek Salad 38
Broiled Salmon with Herb Mustard 39
Country Olive Biscuits 41
Mushroom, Chorizo and Haloumi Tacos 43
Braised Swiss Chard with Currants and Feta 44
Buon Giorno Frittata 45
Cauliflower Couscous 46
Greek-Style Baked Salmon 47
Zucchini Blossoms with Bulgur 48
Turkey Hummus Sliders 50
Warm Olives with Rosemary 52
Grilled Asparagus Salad 53
Cheese, Herb and Sun-Dried Phyllo Rolls 54
Couscous and Bulgur Pilaf 56
Country Style Corn Chowder 58
Chipotle Olive Turkey Chili 59
Louvi 61
Creamy Garlic Pasta with Shrimps and Vegetables 62
Eggplant Pilaf with Pistachios and Cinnamon 64
Chicken Gyros with Cucumber Salsa and Tsatsiki 66
Eggplant Frittata 68
Gnocchi with Zucchini Ribbons and Parsley Brown Butter ... 69
Feta and Marinated Nicoise Olives with Grilled Pitas 71
Spanakorizo 72
Crispy Chicken Stew with Lemon, Artichokes, Capers and Olives 73

Baked Falafel *75*
Courgette and Quinoa-Stuffed Peppers *77*
Garlicky Greek Salad *78*
Grilled Chicken, Red Onion and Mint Kebabs *79*
Chorizo Pilaf *81*
Ravioli and Vegetable Soup *83*
Greek Burger with Arugula, Tomatoes and Feta *84*
Caponata *86*
Greek Mussels and Potato Stew *88*
Mediterranean Quinoa Salad *89*
Spinach with Chili and Lemon Crumbs *91*
Greek Orzo and Shrimp Salad *92*
Tortellini Primavera *94*
Greek Chicken Pasta *96*
Mussels with Tomatoes and Chili *98*
Greek Chicken and Vegetable Ragout *99*
Tuscan-Style Tuna Salad *101*
Chicken Kofte with Zucchini *102*
Spinach and Feta Pita Bake *104*
Baked Parmesan Tomatoes *105*
Chicken Souvlaki *106*
Spice Sweet Roasted Red Pepper Hummus *108*
Paprika Shrimp and Green Bean Sauté *109*
Artichoke and Arugula Pizza with Prosciutto *110*
Bean Bolognese *112*
Greek and Penne Chicken *114*
Catalan Sautéed Polenta and Butter Beans *116*
Seared Mediterranean Tuna Steaks *118*
Mustard-Crusted Salmon *119*
Greek Style Potatoes *120*
Rigatoni with Green Olive-Almond Pesto and Asiago Cheese *121*

Sausage, Mushroom and Spinach Lasagna 122
Greek Tzatziki 124
Garlic-Rosemary Lamb Pita 125
Easy Arugula Salad 126
Smoky Corn and Black Bean Pizza 127
Greek-Style Scampi 128
Pasta Fagioli Soup 129
Italian Egg-Drop Soup 131
Greek-Flavored Turkey Burgers 133
Avocado and Tuna Tapas 135
Corn and Broccoli Calzones 136
Saffron Fish Stew with White Beans 138
Slow Cooker Mediterranean Stew 140
Lemony Asparagus Pasta 142
Halibut with Lemon-Fennel Salad 144
Spanish Cod 146
Easy Salmon Cakes 148
Mediterranean Chicken with Eggplant 150
Turkey Kefta Patties with Cucumber Salad 152
Tabouleh 154
Sweet Sausage Marsala 155
Crisp Lamb Lettuce Wraps 156
Spicy Sage and Olive Hash Brown 158

Conclusion 159

Introduction

I want to thank you and congratulate you for downloading the book, *"Mediterranean Diet"*.

This book will take you to the world of eating healthy and following a strict guideline with the delicious recipes of the Mediterranean Diet.

The Mediterranean Diet is about making the right choice and not cutting courses. It is about being smart about what you eat and not being stingy about what you put into your mouth. It is not starvation—instead, it teaches you to enjoy food, the right way—because, food is love. This book highlights the magnificence of food and the beauty of healthy eating.

Thanks again for downloading this book. I hope you enjoy it!

Where Did the Mediterranean Diet Came From

After the 2nd World War was concluded, Ancel Keys conducted a study that analyzed diets of about 13,000 middle-aged men coming from different countries all over the world. The findings were interesting. Americans were found to be the most well-fed, unfortunately, their hearts were the unhealthiest. On the other hand, a portion of individuals from Crete were found to be the financially poorest of the lot, but their hearts were the healthiest.

The focus on the Mediterranean diet changed since then. Found to have originated from Crete, Greece, Southern Italy and Spain, it is a diet that consists mainly of home-grown and fresh produce—the truest essence of what most people know now as, farm-to-table. It was initially given the nickname, "Diet of the Poor" and was specifically tagged to Portugal, but given the desperate nickname, it was quickly rejected.

In 2013, Mediterranean diet was added by UNESCO to the Representative List of Intangible Cultural Heritage of Humanity and was linked to the cultures of Italy, Morocco, Croatia, Portugal, Spain, Cyprus and Greece.

A classification of Intangible Cultural Heritage is defined as *"Practices, representations, knowledge, skills—as well as instruments, objects, artefacts and cultural spaces therewith—that communities, groups and in some cases, individuals recognize as part of their cultural heritage"* (Source: Wikipedia). The diet qualifies because it involves a specific set of knowledge, rituals, traditions and skills, unique to these regions/countries.

The Science Behind The Mediterranean Diet

The best way to explain the mechanism of the Mediterranean diet is through the so-called French Paradox. A parallel phenomenon exists between the fat diet of Americans and that of Mediterranean. You see, they both consume possibly the same amount of fat. Mediterranean dishes are mostly prepared with abundant use of olive oil and American dishes are popular for its "grease".

In terms of quantity, there is hardly a difference, but when you look at the health of these people, you will find that those who maintain a Mediterranean lifestyle exhibit lower rates of heart disease—while people who enjoyed American diets are the opposite.

It is the battle between good and evil. On one side you have the monosaturated fats and polysaturated fats which are good fats and have the ability to lower LDL cholesterol levels. On the other side you have the trans fats and saturated fats which are bad fats and can bring harm to your body. Mediterranean Diet is all about good fats—it involves a lifestyle of healthy choices.

Quick Tips and Tricks for Everyone

Mediterranean is All Over

The easy mistake is to assume that Mediterranean diets are leaning towards Greek food. No, you have to widen your scope a little more because it is not about a country or specific region. This diet is about the ingredients and this means that you can incorporate tastes from Italian, Turkish, Spanish, Moroccan cuisines and others. Later on, in the final section of this book, a few sample recipes will be provided to you. This will help you understand how vast this truly is.

Bread is Life

Carbohydrates are essential because it is an energy source. Unfortunately, it is often deemed evil by most diets. The Mediterranean diet does not mark carbohydrates sinful, but it teaches you which road to take in terms of selecting the right source. Bread is an important feature in Mediterranean diets, but they urge you to use sources made from whole grains. These sources are rich in protein and minerals.

Fat is not Sinful

Fat is not an enemy—at least not all of them. As a matter of fact, our body needs a certain amount of fat. The Mediterranean diet showcases the good fat which is in olive oil, olives and nuts.

The talk about oil and fat is a complicated one. Be a little careful with vegetable oils because it is not one and the same. There are cold-pressed oils that are high in monosaturated fats (peanut oil and extra virgin olive oil) and there are modern processed oils (safflower oil, cottonseed oil, corn oil, soybean oil, canola oil, sunflower oil and vegetable oil). The purists try to stay clear from industrial processing because they are rich in omega 6, which is bad fat.

Spice is Life

Any cook, novice or expert, know that taste is the key to all successful dishes. The look is only secondary because anyone can puke a disgusting meal, even if it looks awesome. The problem most people have with food that tastes good is that they are sinful. The core of this diet structure relies on spices. Armed with its own health benefits, your coriander, cilantro, rosemary and bay leaves, play gustatory medleys in your mouth.

Wine and Dine

Unless otherwise contraindicated for you, wine will partner well with most Mediterranean dishes and in fact, will enhance its flavors. As long as it is taken in moderation, a glass of wine during a meal is healthy and just fine.

Fish and Mercury

Seafood, especially fish, is a big component of Mediterranean dishes. They are quite healthy but some caution is given because they are sometimes found with traces of mercury. As a safety precaution, note the following:

- Toxicity increases with the size and weight of the fish, so avoid bigger species such as swordfish, shark and king mackerel.
- Always be on the lookout for toxicity reports in the local news, so you know if levels are unsafe and highly critical.
- Keep levels low, at 12 ounces a week, for adults and 6 ounces a week for pregnant women and children.

A Simple Guide to Eating and Shopping Using the Mediterranean Way

With that rundown, you can now head on to the grocery and start shopping. Of course you do not have to get all of these, but if you are set on revamping your life and switching to the Mediterranean lifestyle, this list should help jump start your effort.

1. Dairies: cheese, Greek yogurt, milk
2. Eggs: quail, duck, chicken
3. Extra virgin olive oil
4. Fish and seafood: mackerel, salmon, sardines, trout, tuna, mussels, crab, clams, shrimps, shellfish, etc.
5. Fruits and Berries: apples, oranges, bananas, grapes, pears, strawberries, blueberries, blackberries, peaches, melons, etc.
6. Grains: rye, corn, barley, whole oats, brown rice, etc. (whole grain pasta and bread)
7. Legumes: beans, pulses, lentils, etc.
8. Poultry: chicken, turkey, duck, etc.
9. Nuts: cashew, walnut, almonds, macadamia, hazelnuts, etc.
10. Seeds: pumpkin, sunflower, etc.
11. Spices and condiments: pepper, sea salt, turmeric, cinnamon, basil, rosemary, mint, nutmeg, sage, etc.
12. Vegetables: spinach, carrots, broccoli, onions, garlic, kale, sweet potato, potato, olives, etc. (frozen vegetables are also good, as long as combined with fresh)

Health Benefits of the Mediterranean Diet

The Mediterranean Diet has flourished through the years because of its health benefits. When something is good, it lives on and the most significant thing about this diet is that it has amazing contributions to the body:

- Provides protection against diabetes. This diet is very rich in fiber so it promotes slow digestion. This type of food processing is very healthy because it avoids fluctuations in blood sugar, which leads to Type 2 Diabetes.

- It can help you lose weight healthily. It is not about cutting down on weight and shredding fast. With this diet, you can rest assured that you will be losing weight without compromising your health. Apply this diet with regular exercise and you are well on your way to a fit and healthy lifestyle. You do not have to be counting calories, because the ingredients of Mediterranean dishes are low in calorie. Nevertheless they are filling, so you feel satiated for a long time.

- It's all about the ingredients. Some diets concentrate on cutting this, cutting that, counting calories and so forth. The Mediterranean diet focuses on the food. It focuses on using healthy ingredients so you do not have to worry. It uses olive oil, vegetables, beans, nuts, grains—ingredients that are already healthy on its own. Basically, the core of Mediterranean diet is strong and you cannot go wrong with it.

- Food is fresh. Forget about processed ingredients that are rich in preservatives and all things that are bad for you. The ingredients used in the Mediterranean diet are healthy because they are fresh. You can create meals out of anything lying around in your own kitchen, garden or food stores nearby. It is perfect for someone who is on-the-go and in a tight rush. Get your favorite vegetables and add feta cheese and olive oil, and it's a meal in a flash—all fresh and healthy.

- It is simple to make. You do not really have to be a master chef to even attempt a Mediterranean dish. Many of the dishes simply involve mixing things together in a bowl. It is not labor intensive at all. Once again, the focus is the ingredients and not the sophisticated kitchen skill. Given this, anyone can easily take it on and apply it in their daily lives.

- It is good for the heart. Since the fat used in the Mediterranean diet is the good kind of fat, it can even help decrease levels of bad cholesterol in your body. Even the wine feature of this diet supports heart health, so that is something to delight about.

- It is good against cancer. Cancer remains a fearful enemy for all because the degradation involved is not a life you wish for yourself, or anyone you know. While rather small, the application of a strict Mediterranean diet has been found to be linked to the reduction of deaths due to cancer and even the very onset of the disease.

- Risk reduction for various diseases. With its unique features, the Mediterranean diet has been linked to the reduction of the development of Alzheimer's (due to improvements in blood health and cholesterol levels) and Parkinson's disease (due to good anti-oxidant component, which is known to enhance brain activity).

Getting Started on the Mediterranean Diet

You may still have a few questions about the Mediterranean diet and that's fine. It is better to be inquisitive than to impulsively launch into a brand new lifestyle, that you cannot sustain. That is true for many people—they get so psyched about starting something, but they often find it difficult to commit to the diet.

To avoid that, you need to be fully informed before you take the plunge. The following are the common questions and doubts about the diet. You might have the same thoughts, so pay attention:

1. **Will it be an expensive lifestyle?** It is common thinking that going on a strict Mediterranean diet is expensive. Well, you just have to look at the ingredients; nothing about beans and vegetables is expensive. What is going to happen in the start is a complete overhaul of your kitchen and pantry.

    If it is unhealthily stocked, then you can expect to spend some money acquiring the different spices in the beginning. All start ups involve inventory building and once you are fully assimilated, you will realize the amount of money you are actually saving.

2. **Is carbohydrates really okay?** Anything is okay, just as long as you enjoy it in moderation. Mediterranean meals showcase breads and pasta, but unlike other dishes where a mountain of it is served, they are enjoyed as healthy sides. More so, carbohydrates in Mediterranean diets are in its whole wheat variation.

3. **Is there more to it than just the food?** Of course there is. The most successful diets are those which encourage a holistic and sustainable transformation and the Mediterranean way is all about enjoying food and life. It is a whole experience that is far from fast food or binges.

   As you are about to embark on this change, it is encouraged that you take it on, completely. After all, it is all for your benefit. Mediterranean diets are about sitting down, savoring the food and doing so with friends and family. It is about enjoying and embracing life, healthily.

4. **What's the best way to ease into this diet?** Take it slow. If there is one good advice you can take it is to not jump fully into it, only to quit right away. It is never easy to make changes and this is going to be tough. For a realistic approach, therefore, you can ease into it by first, adding more vegetables to your diet.

   Eventually, you can switch from red meat to lean, stop skipping meals and have your breakfast daily, incorporate seafood into your diet at least twice a week, start avoiding the bad fats and switch to good fat, enjoy fruits more and add more dairy into your diet. When you look at it that way, it does not sound so difficult, huh? The whole transition process will be a fairly bumpy ride, therefore, take it slow.

5. **What quick food substitutes can I have for my staples?** In line with the previous concern of easing in, you can work on your transition by actually substituting specific things into healthier choices. Here are some examples: pudding from whole milk instead of ice cream, quinoa with vegetables instead of fried rice,

whole wheat bread instead of white bread and rolls, fresh vegetable sticks and salsa instead of chips and dips.

6. **Do I have to incorporate exercise?** If you want to truly make good of your effort, you will have to incorporate exercise into your lifestyle. To maximize the benefits of the Mediterranean diet, you need to get a lot of exercise. This is most especially true if you are hoping to lose some weight. You can best achieve that by moving a little and staying active.

100 Mediterranean Diet Recipes

After learning about the Mediterranean diet, it is now time to start preparing meals for you. Contrary to what many people think, the Mediterranean diet is not just about salads, although vegetables are very prominent in the dishes.

Healthy does not have to be boring and you will find out soon enough. You will discover the value of choosing the right ingredients. And then, you will appreciate the value of portions.

Happy eating!

1

Mediterranean Medley Salad

4 Servings

This is a simple salad to make, and it's just as it's called. It's a lovely medley of different vegetables. You can change it with whatever ingredients you have at home, so this recipe actually gives you much freedom. Choose your favorite vegetables and let it play a symphony in your mouth.

Ingredients

- 1 tbsp balsamic vinegar
- ½ cup basil leaves, torn
- 2 ounces feta cheese, crumbled
- ¼ cup kalamata olives, sliced
- 4 cups vegetables, roughly chopped (red onions, carrots, tomatoes, cucumber, zucchini, red or green bell pepper)
- 2 tbsp extra virgin olive oil
- 1 pinch of salt and pepper

Instructions

1. In a bowl, combine all the ingredients together.
2. Toss it well, making sure to coat all the vegetables with dressing to spread the flavour.

2
Fluffy Strawberry Buckwheat Pancakes

5 servings

Today's breakfast is going to be an interesting one. The recipe makes use of buckwheat but if you have a hard time finding some, whole wheat will be fine. Feel free to substitute the strawberries for another fruit.

Ingredients
- butter
- 1 egg
- maple syrup
- ¾ cup milk
- 1 cup buckwheat pancake mix (or whole wheat)
- 1 cup fresh strawberries
- 1 ½ cups yogurt

Instructions
1. In a bowl, combine the egg, yogurt, milk and pancake mix.
2. Mix it well until the batter is fluffy.
3. In a skillet, heat butter and use a ladle for one portion of pancake mix.
4. Cook one side until bubbles are form on the surface. Flip to the other side.
5. Serve it with strawberries and maple syrup on top.

3

Artichokes Provencal

4 servings

What a bowl of pure goodness and flavor. The artichoke hearts will definitely showcase the amazing lemon-basil zest. It is a treat, not just for the eyes, but for the heart.

Ingredients

- 2 packs artichoke hearts
- basil
- 2 cloves garlic, chopped
- 1 strip lemon zest
- ½ onion, chopped
- olives, chopped
- 1 tbsp olive oil
- 2 tomatoes, chopped
- 3 tbsp water
- ½ cup white wine
- salt and pepper, to taste

Instructions

1. In a skillet, heat oil and sauté garlic and onion for about five minutes.
2. Add white wine and cook until it is reduced by half.
3. Add the tomatoes and artichokes. Let it simmer for a while.
4. Add the water and lemon zest. Add salt, to taste.
5. Just before you finish cooking, add the olives and basil. Season with salt and pepper.

4

Fattoush Salad

6 servings

This is a simple salad dish that plays with different colors. The lime-vinaigrette is just to-die-for with its very characteristic taste.

Ingredients

- 1 cucumber, chopped
- 1 heart romaine lettuce, chopped
- olive oil
- green onions, chopped
- 1 cup parsley, chopped
- 2 loaves pita bread
- 5 radishes, stems removed and chopped
- ½ tsp sumac
- 5 roma tomatoes, chopped
- salt and pepper, to taste

lime vinaigrette:

- ½ ground all spice
- ½ tsp cinnamon
- 1 ½ lime juice
- ½ cup olive oil
- 1 tsp ground sumac
- salt and pepper, to taste

Instructions

1. In a toaster, heat the pita bread until it is crisp but do not wait for it to brown.
2. In a pan, heat oil and break the pita bread into pieces and let it fry. Season with salt and pepper. Then add ½ tsp sumac. Set aside.
3. In a bowl, bring together the tomatoes, cucumber, lettuce, radish, green onions and parsley.
4. Make the vinaigrette. In a bowl, bring together the lime juice, spices and olive oil.
5. Combine everything in a large bowl and toss it well. Make sure all the vegetables and pita are coated evenly with the dressing. Add more sumac, to taste.

5

Balsamic & Parmesan Roasted Cauliflower

4 servings

The great thing about cauliflower is that it is able to carry different flavors. The texture is lovely and when roasted, you will be surprised at how amazingly it can transform.

Ingredients

- 2 tbsp balsamic vinegar
- 8 cups cauliflower florets
- ½ cup parmesan cheese, grated
- 1 tsp marjoram
- 2 tbsp extra virgin olive oil
- salt and pepper, to taste

Instructions

1. Preheat oven to 450°F.
2. In a bowl, mix together the olive oil, marjoram, cauliflower, salt and pepper.
3. Lay everything on a baking sheet and pop it in the oven. Let it bake until bottom starts to brown and take it out.
4. Add vinegar and cheese on top of the roasted cauliflower and toss everything. Pop it back into the oven. Let it cook until the cheese melt.

6

Chickpea Spread

2 servings

If you are fond of snacking and would like to have a healthy substitute for your usual choices, here is a simple chickpea spread recipe that you can use for sandwiches, crackers and vegetables.

Ingredients

- 7.5 ounces chickpea
- ¼ tsp cumin (optional)
- 1 clove garlic, minced
- 1 tbsp lemon juice
- 2 tsp olive oil

Instructions

1. In a bowel, mash the chickpeas using a fork.
2. Add olive oil, garlic and lemon juice. Season it with salt.
3. Add cumin if you wish to give this dip a characteristic kick.

7

Spicy Escarole with Garlic

4 servings

Here's a very interesting way to enjoy escarole. If you want more flavor than your usual salad dish, here's a fantastic recipe that showcases a spicy garlic kick.

Ingredients

- head of escarole
- 2 garlic cloves, minced
- olive oil
- 1 pinch red pepper flakes

Instructions

1. In skillet, heat oil and sauté garlic until they are golden.
2. Add a red pepper flakes and stir it with the oil to blend the flavors.
3. Add the head of escarole, by increments. Season it with salt and pepper.
4. Cover the skillet and wait until the escarole are wilted.

8

Barley, Feta and Pear Salad

2 servings

Here is a light vegetable and fruit salad that's definitely delicious. It is high in fiber and the interesting textures in this dish will give you a true adventure in your mouth.

Ingredients

- 1/3 cup pearl barley
- 1 celery rib, diced
- ¼ cup feat cheese
- 1 tbsp lemon juice
- 1 ½ tbsp extra-virgin olive oil
- ½ cup parsley, chopped
- ½ firm pear, peeled, cored and diced
- ½ head radicchio, diced
- 3 tbsp walnuts

Instructions

1. Preheat oven to 375°F.
2. In a sauce pan, boil barley until it's tender. Drain.
3. In a baking pan, toast walnuts until golden brown.
4. In a bowl, combine the barley with feta, nuts, celery, parsley, pear, radicchio, oil and lemon juice. Season with salt and pepper, to taste.
5. Toss well. Make sure to coat everything evenly

9

Bourtheto Fish Stew

3 servings

This unique Italian fish dish is given a very unique touch and will be a delight to try, especially for the first time. It is simple and not at all demanding, so you can whip it up with much ease.

Ingredients

- 1/8 tsp cayenne
- 4 cod fillets
- ¼ cup olive oil
- 1 ¼ cups onions, sliced
- ½ tsp paprika
- 1 cup water
- salt and pepper, to taste

Instructions

1. In a pan, heat the oil and sauté the onions.
2. Add the water, cayenne and paprika. Season with salt and pepper. Let it boil and simmer until the onions have softened.
3. Add the cod and let the fish simmer until it is thoroughly cooked.
4. Serve with the onions on top of the fish.

10

Creamy and Crunchy Cereal Yogurt

2 servings

Do you love your cereal? Here is an easy cereal yogurt dish that is perfect for breakfast. You can prepare this a night before to be enjoyed in the morning—or rush with it on the day. It won't take so long to prepare. Feel free to add fresh or dried fruits for more flavor.

Ingredients

- 1 cup cereal (Cheerios, Raisin Bran)
- 3 tbsp walnuts, chopped
- 6 ounces yogurt

Instructions

1. In a bowl, mix yogurt with your choice of cereal. Choose the one that's crunchy so it doesn't get soggy right away, with the yogurt.
2. Add walnuts and mix it well.

11

Bass Agrodolce with Spaghetti Squash and Mushrooms

4 servings

What a lovely way to enjoy fish? The use of the squash is definitely entertaining. Who said spaghetti cannot be the healthiest food you can have?

Ingredients

- agrodolce sauce
- 2 striped bass fillets
- 1 head garlic, peeled
- 5 tbsp extra-virgin olive oil
- 12 ounces mixed mushrooms, roughly chopped
- 1 pinch red pepper flakes
- 4 sprigs rosemary
- 3 tbsp sugar
- 1 squash
- ¼ cup red wine vinegar
- 2 cups cherry tomatoes
- salt and pepper, to taste

Instructions

1. Preheat oven to 375°F.
2. In a pan, heat oil and sauté the garlic, pepper flakes and rosemary until the garlic is tender. Set it aside.
3. In the same pan, add vinegar and sugar. Mix them together until you achieve a syrupy consistency.

4. Cut the squash lengthwise, removing the seeds, and brush it with garlic oil. Season it with salt and pepper.
5. In a baking dish, lay the squash and let it bake until it is tender. Take it out and create squash strands using a fork. Season it with salt and pepper.
6. In a skillet, heat oil and sauté the mushrooms until it is browned. Set it aside.
7. Add the tomatoes and toss it until they begin to blister.
8. Add the agrodolce sauce and return the mushrooms.
9. In a sauce pan, bring water to boil.
10. Season the fish with salt and pepper. Let it steam.
11. Arrange everything on the plate. Lay the fish. Add the squash on the side with the tomatoes and mushroom. Cover it with agrodolce sauce and top it with caramelized garlic.

12

Mussels Marinara di Amore

4 servings

If you fancy seafood, this lovely recipe makes use of mussels. The marinara sauce offers an interesting pool of flavors for the mussels and gives the pasta dish a truly interesting taste.

Ingredients

- ½ tsp basil
- 1 clove garlic, mince
- 1 lemon, wedges
- 1 pound mussels, cleaned and debearded
- 1 tbsp olive oil
- ½ tsp oregano
- 8 ounces whole wheat linguini pasta
- 1 pinch pepper flakes, crushed
- 14.5 ounces can tomatoes, crushed
- ¼ cup white wine

Instructions

1. Cook the pasta accordingly. Set aside.
2. In a skillet, heat oil and sauté garlic.
3. Add the tomatoes, basil, pepper flakes and oregano. Reduce the heat and let them simmer.
4. Add wine and increase the heat once again. Wait for the mussels to cook and open. That should be about 3 to 5 minutes.
5. Transfer the sauce over the pasta. Garnish with parsley and place lemon wedges on the side.

13

Chicken Piccata with Pasta and Mushrooms

4 servings

This is a simple, yet tasty chicken dish with a very characteristic lemon-caper sauce that is just unforgettable. This recipe specifically uses chicken but feel free to substitute the meat with fish or shrimps.

Ingredients

- 2 tsp butter
- 2 tbsp capers, rinsed
- 4 chicken breast fillets
- 2 cups chicken broth
- 1/3 cup all purpose flour
- 3 cloves of garlic, minced
- 2 tbsp lemon juice
- 3 tbsp extra-virgin olive oil, divided
- 10 ounces mushrooms, sliced
- ¼ cup parsley, chopped
- 6 ounces whole wheat anger hair pasta
- ½ cup white wine
- salt and pepper, to taste

Instructions

1. Cook pasta accordingly. Set aside.
2. In a shallow bowl, whisk about 5 tsp of flour with the broth until they are properly mixed.

3. Season chicken with salt and pepper, then dredge it with flour.

4. In a skillet, heat oil and cook the chicken until it is golden brown. Take away from heat and set aside.

5. In another skillet, heat oil and sauté mushrooms until they release their juices and are properly browned. Transfer them on a plate.

6. Using the same skillet, heat the wine and garlic together, until the wine is reduced. Add the broth-flour mixture prepared earlier. Add the lemon juice and season it with salt. Cook everything until the sauce thickens.

7. Add the parsley, butter, capers and the rest of the mushrooms.

8. Add the pasta in the pan and serve it with the chicken. Mix all of it together.

14

Mediterranean Sweet and Sour Chicken

4 servings

Sweet and sour is very oriental in descent but who said that Mediterranean dishes have to be confined to a specific taste characteristic?

Ingredients

- 1 bag baby arugula
- ½ cup chicken broth
- 8 skinless chicken, thigh
- 2 tsp cornstarch
- 2 clove garlic
- ¾ cup Mission figs
- ¼ cup olives
- 2 tsp olive oil
- 2 tsp brown sugar
- ½ cup red wine vinegar
- salt and pepper, to taste

Instructions

1. In a skillet, heat oil and add chicken. Season it with salt. Cook the chicken until it is browned. Set it aside.
2. In the same skillet, sauté the garlic.
3. In a cup, combine the vinegar, broth, cornstarch and sugar. Add this to the garlic. Cook until the sauce thickens.
4. Add the figs and olives.
5. Bring back the chicken and let it simmer to absorb the flavor.
6. Serve with arugula on top.

15

Pineapple Smoothie

1 serving

There are some days when you will be asking for something truly fresh and light. So why not have a smoothie? This pineapple smoothie is truly refreshing and it is going to be perfect for a hot morning.

Ingredients

- ½ oranges
- ½ cup pineapple chunks
- 6 ounces yogurt

Instructions

1. In a food processor, let all the fruits and yogurt blend well together.
2. By increments, add ice cubes until you achieve the consistency you want.

16

Mussels with Potatoes and Olives

4 servings

Feast on this mighty mussels dish that features a generous selection of spices. Let the flavors take you to a place you haven't been to, ever before.

Ingredients

- 1 pinch allspice
- 1 pinch cayenne pepper
- 2 cloves garlic, sliced
- 2 ¼ mussels, scrubbed
- 2/3 cup green olives, pitted
- 2 tbsp extra-virgin olive oil
- 1 onion, sliced
- ½ cup parsley, roughly chopped
- ½ tsp paprika
- 1 potato, chunks
- 14.5 ounces canned tomatoes, diced
- salt and pepper, to taste

Instructions

1. In a bowl, microwave the potatoes, until they are tender. Seal it well. Drain.
2. In a pot, heat oil and sauté onions and garlic, until they are tender and brown.
3. Add the cayenne pepper, paprika and allspice. Add the potatoes and everything. Simmer for about 3 minutes.

4. Add the tomatoes and cook everything until the potatoes are perfect.
5. Add the mussels, parsley and olives. Cover it and let the mussels cook until they open. Make sure to discard the shells that did not open.

17

Cicoria e Fagiolo

4 servings

If the name confused you a little, that just means chicory and beans. This very simple lean dish is surprisingly substantial and will make you smile. It is simple. It is healthy. It is all you need for a light meal.

Ingredients

- 15 ounces cannellini beans
- 2 heads chicory
- 3 cloves garlic
- olive oil
- 1 pinch dried pepper flakes
- salt to taste

Instructions

1. In a bowl, put salted water and boil the chicory until it is tender. This should take about 10 minutes. Drain and set it aside. Chop roughly, once cooled.
2. In pan, heat oil and sauté garlic until it is brown. Add the red pepper flakes. Remove the garlic and set it aside.
3. Add the chicory to the pan and let it simmer until it has absorbed the flavour of the oil.
4. Add the beans and add some more water if needed. Season with salt.

18

Savory Pancake with Lemon-Dill Yogurt

2 servings

Have you ever had a savory pancake? Here's a lovely way to enjoy your breakfast favorite.

Ingredients

- 1 ounce cheddar cheese, shredded
- ½ tsp dill
- 4 egg whites
- 1 tbsp lemon juice
- olive oil
- ½ cup dry quick oats
- ½ cup scallions
- ½ cup Greek yogurt
- salt and pepper, to taste

Instructions

1. Prepare the lemon-dill sauce by combining the lemon juice, yogurt and dill together in a bowl. Mix it well and then set it aside.
2. In a bowl, combine the egg whites, oats, scallions and cheese. Season with salt and pepper.
3. In a pan, pour a ladle of the batter and let it cook. Flip it once the other side is done.
4. Serve with a dollop of lemon-dill sauce.

19

Chicken and Spinach Wrap

1 serving

This is a simple and perfect on-the-go snack if you want something light but definitely satisfying.

Ingredients

- 4 ounces grilled chicken breast
- 2 tbsp red onions, sliced
- 1 bunch baby spinach leaves
- 2 tbsp tomato, chopped
- 1 whole grain tortilla
- 2 tbsp. red wine vinaigrette

Instructions

1. Take a tortilla and stuff it generously with spinach.
2. Add the tomatoes and onions.
3. Finally, add the strips of grilled chicken breast.
4. Sprinkle it with red wine vinaigrette.

20

Broccoli Rabe with Cherry Peppers

4 servings

You may not be very familiar with the use of broccoli rabe, but there is always a first time. This is a simple vegetable dish that can easily become a favorite.

Ingredients

- 2 bunches broccoli rabe
- 2 cloves garlic, sliced
- 1 tbsp olive oil
- Parmesan cheese, shaved
- ¼ cup cherry peppers (from jar)
- 2 tbsp liquid from cheery pepper jar

Instructions

1. Steam the broccoli rabe until they are tender.
2. In a pot, heat oil and sauté garlic until they are golden.
3. Add the cherry peppers and the cherry pepper liquid.
4. Add the steamed broccoli rabe. Season with salt and pepper.
5. Drizzle with olive oil and serve with parmesan cheese, on top.

21

Beet, Chickpea and Almond Dip with Pita Chips

2 servings

Who said snacking is bad? It is not a sin to snack. You just really have to know what food to choose. So how about a healthy snack that can truly bring a smile to your face? This pita and dip combo is bound to please. All the more, it is healthy and guilt-free.

Ingredients

- ¼ cup almond, slivered
- 15 ½ ounces garbanzo beans
- 8 ounces beet, cubed
- 5 garlic cloves, peeled
- ¾ cup extra-virgin olive oil
- 6 pita breads
- 1 ½ tbsp red wine vinegar

Instructions

1. In a saucepan, boil beet until it is tender.
2. Drain and let it run in a food processor. Add the garbanzo beans, almonds, oil, and garlic and blend everything well until it is smooth.
3. Add the red wine and blend even further. Season with salt and pepper, to taste. Chill in the refrigerator. Serve at room temperature with a platter of pita bread.

22

Mediterranean Greek Salad

8 servings

This is a very simple salad with taste that relies on the freshness of the ingredients. There is very little oil used, just enough to add some moisture to the vegetables, so you can enjoy the ingredients in the rawness of their taste.

Ingredients

- 1 ½ cups crumbled feta cheese
- 3 cucumbers, seeded and sliced
- 1 cup pitted black olives, sliced
- ½ red onion, sliced
- 3 cups roma tomatoes
- 1/3 cup sundried tomatoes, set aside the oil

Instructions

1. In a bowl, combine all the ingredients together.
2. Get the reserved sundried tomato oil that you set aside and pour it into the ingredients. Make sure to coat everything well.

23

Broiled Salmon with Herb Mustard

6 servings

This is a very simple, yet flavorful way to enjoy salmon. The best way to showcase fish is really not to smother it with too much flavour and this does that perfectly.

Ingredients

- 2 cloves garlic
- 6 lemon wedges
- 2 tbsp Dijon mustard
- 2 tbsp whole grain mustard
- olive oil cooking spray
- 1 tbsp extra-virgin olive oil
- ¾ tsp rosemary, finely chopped
- 6 salmon fillets
- ¾ tsp thyme, finely chopped
- 1 tbsp dry white wine
- salt and pepper, to taste

Instructions

1. In a food processor, mix the rosemary, garlic, thyme, oil, wine, Dijon mustard and 1 tbsp whole grain mustard together. Make sure that it is properly combined. Add the remaining whole grain mustard. Set it aside.
2. Preheat the broiler.

3. Grease baking sheet and lay the salmon fillet. Season it with salt and pepper. Let the fish broil for about 2 minutes.

4. With a spoon, spread mustard sauce on the fish and continue to broil it until they are golden brown.

24

Country Olive Biscuits

2 servings

If you would rather have biscuits instead of store bought bread, here is a magnificent biscuit recipe that will win everyone's praise.

Ingredients

- 2 tsp baking powder
- ½ tsp baking soda
- 1/3 cup unsalted butter
- 2 cups cake flour
- ½ cup cheddar cheese, shredded
- 3 ounces ham, thinly sliced
- ¾ cup reduced fat buttermilk
- 1 tbsp honey mustard
- ½ cup olives, chopped
- ½ tsp salt

Instructions

1. Preheat oven to 475ºF.
2. In a bowl, mix together the flour, baking soda and baking powder.
3. Add the butter, cutting it with a fork.
4. Add olives and cheddar cheese.
5. Pour the buttermilk into the bowl and knead everything together until it is doughy.

6. Using a biscuit cutter, form biscuits and lay them on a baking sheet.
7. Bake until it is golden brown.
8. Serve with mustard and ham.

25

Mushroom, Chorizo and Haloumi Tacos

8 servings

Here is an amazing twist to the Mexican favorite. The combination of chorizo, mushroom and cheese will definitely feel like a fiesta in your mouth. Make sure to enjoy every bite with a smile.

Ingredients

- 200g haloumi cheese, sliced
- chillies, chopped
- 1 chorizo, sliced
- coriander, chopped
- 500g button mushrooms
- 3 tbsp olive oil
- 1 pinch oregano
- 8 whole wheat tortilla
- salt and pepper, to taste

Instructions

1. Preheat oven to 400ºF.
2. In a bowl, combine the oil, mushrooms and oregano. Season it with salt and pepper. Transfer into a baking tray and pop it in the oven. Cook until the mushrooms have browned.
3. In a pan, heat oil and cook the chorizo until it is crispy. Set aside.
4. In a bowl, combine the chorizo and the mushroom mixture. Add the cheese and mix it all together.
5. Once mixed, assemble the taco using the heated tortilla. Just pack it with enough filling and fold it.

26

Braised Swiss Chard with Currants and Feta

4 servings

Here is a unique salad dish that will truly captivate your senses. First of all, the colors are interesting with the many contrasting details you will find on your plate. Then you get the amazing texture of the different ingredients, fighting over the nerve endings on your tongue. Finally, you let the taste play music in your mouth and it is such a great party.

Ingredients

- 1 bunch Swiss chard, coarsely chop
- 1/3 cup feat cheese, crumbed
- 3 tbsp dried currants
- 1 garlic clove, finely chopped
- 2 tbsp olive oil
- 1/3 cup water
- salt and pepper, to taste

Instructions

1. In a pot, heat oil and sauté garlic until it is golden.
2. Add the chard ribs and stems. Season with salt and pepper.
3. Add currants and cook until it is plump.
4. Add water, chard leaves and cook in high heat or until the leaves are tender.
5. Remove from heat and add feta cheese.

27

Buon Giorno Frittata

3 servings

Here is a very packed breakfast dish that is more than just healthy. It is filling. Pair it with bread or have it on its own. It is wonderful on the plate and even more so, in the mouth.

Ingredients

- ¼ cup basil, shredded
- ½ cup Fontina cheese, grated
- 6 eggs, beaten
- 2 tbsp milk
- 6 ounces black olives
- 1/8 tsp olive oil
- 1 cup onions, chopped
- ½ cup roasted red bell peppers, sliced
- 2 cups zucchini, sliced
- salt and pepper, to taste

Instructions

1. Preheat oven to 400°F.
2. In a bowl, combine the eggs, milk and basil together. Season it with salt and pepper. Set it aside.
3. In a pan, heat oil and sauté onions and zucchini until the zucchini is tender.
4. Add the olives and red bell peppers. Take it away from the heat, then pour in the beaten egg mixture over the vegetables. Let it cover the pan evenly.
5. Return it to the heat and let the frittata cook.
6. Sprinkle it with cheese and pop it into the oven.
7. Cook it until it is slightly browned.

28

Cauliflower Couscous

4 servings

Are you looking for a perfect rice substitute? Here is an amazing couscous dish that is given more character by the texture provided by the cauliflower.

Ingredients

- 3 cups cauliflower florets
- 1 pinch cinnamon
- 1 ½ cups couscous
- ½ cup dates, chopped
- olive oil
- 1 shallot, sliced
- red wine vinegar
- salt and pepper, to taste

Instructions

1. Cook the couscous accordingly. Drain and rinse in cold water. Drizzle with olive oil and toss it well.

2. In a pan, heat oil and cook the cauliflower. Season it with salt and pepper.

3. Add dates and a pinch of cinnamon. Let everything cook. Combine this mixture with the couscous.

4. Drizzle with red wine vinegar and top it with parsley. Season with salt and pepper, to taste.

29

Greek-Style Baked Salmon

8 servings

This is a very light and tasty fish dish. Salmon is best when baked because its meat becomes tender and tasty. The tomato salsa combines well with the salmon and creates a fresh taste in the mouth.

Ingredients

- 1 tbsp basil, chopped
- ½ feta cheese, crumbled
- 1 tbsp lemon juice
- 4 kalamata olives, sliced
- ¼ cup olive oil
- ¼ red onion, diced
- 8 salmon fillets with skin
- 4 roma tomatoes, diced

Instructions

1. Preheat oven to 350°F.
2. Spread the sides of the salmon fillets with olive oil and with the skin down, lay them all on a baking dish.
3. Lay the other ingredients all over the dish along with the salmon fillets and sprinkle the lot with lemon juice.
4. Pop the dish into the oven and cook everything for about 20 minutes or until the flakes fray easily.

30

Zucchini Blossoms with Bulgur

6 servings

What an interesting use of the famous Mediterranean staple, bulgur. It is served with the very attractive zucchini blossoms. You wouldn't know whether to eat it or marvel at its beauty.

Ingredients

- 1 cup bulgur
- ½ tsp chilli pepper
- 1 cup chives, chopped
- ½ cup dill, chopped
- 3 cloves garlic, minced
- 3 tbsp mint, chopped
- ½ cup pine nuts (optional)
- 1 cup olive oil
- 1 cup onion, chopped
- 2/3 cup raisins (optional)
- 1 ½ cups water
- 1 cup zucchini, grated
- 20-25 zucchini blossoms
- salt and pepper, to taste

Instructions

1. Preheat oven to 375°F.
2. In a skillet, heat oil and sauté the onions, garlic and chives. Let everything soften.

3. Add the zucchini, chilli pepper, raisins and bulgur. Add the water and reduce heat. If needed, add more water.

4. Add the mint, dill and pine nuts. Remove from heat. Season with salt and pepper to taste.

5. Spoon the filling into the zucchini blossoms and stuff it generously. Then fold the sides to shut it clean and lay them on a casserole. Cover the stuffed blossoms with water and oil. Cover and pop it in the oven. Cook for about an hour or until most of the liquid has been absorbed.

31

Turkey Hummus Sliders

6 servings

Would you like a fancy turkey extravaganza? Sliders are mini burgers, but there is nothing small about the massive taste of this dish.

Ingredients

- ½ cup feta cheese, crumbled
- 2 tsp coriander
- 1 cucumber, diced
- 1 cup hummus
- 1 tsp mint
- 4 tbsp extra-virgin olive oil
- ½ cup parsley, chopped
- 16 mini whole wheat pita pockets
- 3 roma tomatoes, sliced
- 1 ½ pounds ground turkey
- 2 tbsp red wine vinegar
- salt and pepper, to taste

Instructions

1. In a bowl, combine the cucumber, feta cheese, olive oil and mint together. Season it with salt and pepper. Let it stand in the refrigerator.

2. In another bowl, mix the ½ cup hummus, turkey, coriander and parsley. Season it with pepper. Mix well and make patties.

3. In a skillet, heat oil and cook the patties thoroughly.
4. In a new bowl, get the remaining hummus and mix it with hot water. Spread hummus on the pita bread and fill each one with tomato slices, turkey and the cucumber mixture.

32

Warm Olives with Rosemary

2 servings

This is a unique starter or a side. It is very simple but it aims to surprise the palate.

Ingredients

- ¼ tsp fennel seeds
- 4 ounces black olives
- 4 ounces green olives
- ¼ cup olive oil
- 1 pinch crushed red pepper
- 1 sprig rosemary

Instructions

1. In a skillet, heat oil and combine all the ingredients together.
2. Cook everything well until the olives start to brown.

33

Grilled Asparagus Salad

2 servings

The best thing about asparagus is that it is all texture but its versatility makes it a perfect vegetable to blend with interesting flavors. The texture it offers is good for grilling, so enjoy.

Ingredients

- 1 pound asparagus
- 2 tbsp parmesan cheese, grated
- 1 ½ tbsp lemon juice
- 1 cup black olives, pitted
- 2 tbsp olive oil
- 2 tsp red onion, diced
- 2 tbsp Dijon mustard
- salt and pepper, to taste

Instructions

1. In a bowl, combine the asparagus with 1 tbsp oil and toss it well. Season it with salt and pepper.
2. Grill the asparagus until browned.
3. Using the same bowl, add the lemon juice, red onions and the remaining olive oil. Toss everything well and set it aside.
4. Combine the asparagus with the vinaigrette. Add the olives and top it with parmesan cheese.

34

Cheese, Herb and Sun-Dried Phyllo Rolls

4 Servings

This phyllo roll is for the cheese-lover. It is a truly indulgent but health-conscious dish. It showcases interesting tastes that will melt in the mouth in a very unique way.

Ingredients

- ¼ feta cheese, crumbled
- ¾ cup aged kefalotyri cheese, grated
- ¾ cup kasseri cheese, grated
- 1 egg
- 1 tsp marjoram, chopped
- extra-virgin olive oil
- 8 sheets phyllo pastry
- 2 tbsp sun-dried tomatoes, finely chopped
- 2 tsp thyme
- pepper to taste

Instructions

1. In a bowl, whisk egg well until it becomes frothy.
2. Add tomatoes, cheese, marjoram, thyme and pepper. Set aside and chill in the refrigerator.
3. Stack the phyllo sheets and cut them lengthwise.
4. Brush each strip with oil and place a heaping of the chilled cheese filling on the sheets. Fold it to cover and

roll it until it is properly sealed. Brush the entire phyllo with oil. Set aside and refrigerate.

5. Preheat oven at 350°F.
6. Pop the rolled up pastry and let it bake until golden brown.

35

Couscous and Bulgur Pilaf

6 servings

Enjoy this as an appetizer or a light meal. It is a simple couscous and bulgur dish which is quite basic but it is seriously healthy. The flavor is very interesting and is very characteristic of a classic Mediterranean meal.

Ingredients

- 2 cups vegetable broth
- 1 cup bulgur
- 1 tbsp chives, chopped
- ½ cup couscous
- 2 tbsp. olive oil
- 1 ¾ cup onions, chopped
- 1 tbsp parsley, chopped
- ¼ tsp rosemary, chopped

Instructions

1. In a saucepan, heat 2 tbsp oil and sauté onions until they become golden.

2. Add the bulgur and 1 ½ cups of vegetable broth and let everything simmer. Cook until liquid has reduced and the bulgur is tender. Remove from heat and fluff the bulgur with a fork.

3. In another saucepan, heat the rest of the vegetable broth and let it simmer.

4. Add the oil and couscous. Cook this until couscous is tender. Fluff it with a fork.
5. In a large bowl, combine the bulgur and the couscous. Top it with rosemary, chives and parsley. Season it with salt and pepper.

36

Country Style Corn Chowder

6 servings

Fancy of having some soup today? This is a simple but very flavorful chowder recipe that is definitely healthy.

Ingredients

- 1 tbsp unsalted butter
- 4 cups corn kernels
- ½ cup heavy cream
- 2 tbsp dill, chopped
- 2 cups leeks, diced
- 1 cup black olives wedged
- 1 ½ cup potatoes, diced
- 1 cup red bell peppers, diced
- 3 cups chicken stock

Instructions

1. In a saucepot, heat butter. Cook the leeks until they are tender.
2. Add the potatoes, red bell peppers and corn. Cook everything for about 4 minutes.
3. Add the chicken stock and cream. Bring everything to a boil. Cover and let things simmer.
4. Add the dill and simmer for about 5 minutes.
5. Let this cool and then let it run in a food processor. Puree this soup mixture.
6. Return everything into the pot. Add the olives and sprinkle it with cheddar cheese.

37

Chipotle Olive Turkey Chili

6 servings

If you are expecting a few guests tonight, this is a lovely dish to serve. It is definitely interesting with the use of chipotle, so be prepared for your senses to travel.

Ingredients

- 2 ½ cups pinto beans
- 1 cup amber beer
- 2 ½ cups broth
- 1 tbsp canola oil
- 4 tsp chipotle chilli powder
- 1 tsp cumin
- 1 tbsp garlic, minced
- 1 ½ green bell peppers, diced
- 1 cup black olives, halved
- 1 onion, diced
- 1/3 cup parsley
- 3 tbsp tomato paste
- 1 pound ground turkey
- salt and pepper, to taste

Instructions

1. In saucepan, heat oil and sauté onions. Add the ground turkey and cook thoroughly.

2. Add the green bell peppers and garlic.

3. Add the broth, olives, beans, tomato paste, chilli powder, cumin and beer. Season it with salt and pepper. Bring everything to a boil. Cover and let it simmer.
4. Uncover and add parsley. Cook it for about 5 minutes then serve, while hot.

38

Louvi

5 servings

What exactly is a louvi? Well outside of Cyprus, Louvi is basically called Blackeyed Peas with Chard and Blackeyed Peas Salad with Avocado. This particular dish is also popular in Greece and is given the name, louvi xero or louvi fresko. It is a very nutritious dish that is quite easy to prepare.

Ingredients

- 3 cups chard
- 1 tbsp dill
- 1 clove garlic, finely chopped
- 1/3 cup lemon juice
- ¼ cup olive oil
- 1 onion, finely chopped
- 1 spring onion, finely chopped
- 3 tbsp parsley, finely chopped
- 250g blackeyed peas
- 4 cups water
- salt and pepper, to taste

Instructions

1. In a pot, boil the blackeyed peas until they are soft. This should take about 15 minutes. Drain and set aside.
2. In a pan, heat oil. Sauté the garlic and onion then add the chard. Stir generously.
3. Add the beans. Season with salt and pepper to taste.
4. Add the lemon juice and water. Let it simmer in low heat.

39

Creamy Garlic Pasta with Shrimps and Vegetables

4 servings

This is such a unique pasta dish with a creamy yogurt base. It looks so simple but the collection of ingredients is interesting enough to create a party on a plate and then into your palates true satisfaction.

Ingredients

- 1 bunch asparagus, trimmed and sliced
- 1 red bell pepper, thinly sliced
- 3 cloves garlic, chopped
- 3 tbsp lemon juice
- 1 tbsp extra-virgin olive oil
- ¼ cup parsley, chopped
- 1 cup peas
- 12 ounces raw shrimps, peeled, deveined and cut
- 6 ounces whole wheat spaghetti
- 1 ½ cups yogurt
- ¼ cup pine nuts, toasted (optional)
- salt and pepper, to taste

Instructions

1. Cook pasta accordingly but just before it is cooked, add the shrimps, bell peppers, asparagus and peas. Drain the water once the pasta is cooked.
2. In a bowl, mash the garlic to form a paste from it.

3. Add parsley, lemon juice, olive oil, yogurt and pepper. Add this mixture to the pasta and toss everything together.

4. You may or may not top the pasta with pine nuts, as garnish.

40

Eggplant Pilaf with Pistachios and Cinnamon

6 servings

Here is a very creative but truly satisfying pilaf dish. The mix of contrasting flavors will probably make your eyebrows raise, but wait to be surprised at how beautifully they go together. Enjoy this as a side or an appetizer.

Ingredients

- ¾ tsp cinnamon
- ¼ dill, chopped
- 1 eggplant, cubed
- ¼ cup extra-virgin olive oil
- ¼ pistachios, coarsely chopped
- ¼ cup raisins or currants
- 1 cup basmati rice
- 1 tomato, peeled, seeded and finely chopped
- 1 ½ cups water
- salt to taste

Instructions

1. Soak eggplant in a bowl for about 30 minutes. Drain and squeeze it to remove the water and let it dry.
2. In a skillet, heat 2 tsp oil and sauté the eggplant until it is brown. Set aside to cool.
3. In the same skillet, use the remaining oil and sauté onions until softened.

4. Add rice and cook for about 2 minutes, then add water, cinnamon and salt. Let it boil, then reduce heat and cook until rice is tender.

5. Fluff the cooked rice. Add the tomato and the eggplant. Cover and let it simmer.

6. Add the dill and mix it well.

7. Serve on platter with pistachios on top.

41

Chicken Gyros with Cucumber Salsa and Tsatsiki

4 servings

This is an interesting gyro recipe that you can enjoy leisurely or take with you, to-go. The flavors and textures are simple but it is all that you will need for a nice busy day.

Ingredients

- 12 ounces naan bread (or 4 pita rounds)
- ½ roast chicken, shredded
- 2 cucumbers, divided
- 5 garlic cloves, minced and divided
- ½ head iceberg lettuce, thinly sliced
- 1 tsp lemon juice, divided
- ¼ cup mint, chopped
- ¼ cup extra-virgin olive oil
- 1 red onion, thinly sliced
- 1 tsp oregano
- 1/3 cup parsley, chopped
- 1 tsp rosemary, crumbled
- 1 pint grape tomatoes, quartered
- 1 ½ cups Greek yogurt

Instructions

1. Preheat broiler.
2. Divide the cucumber and set one aside. To make the tsatsiki, combine cucumber with the yogurt and ½ tsp

lemon juice. Add 1/3 of the portion of the garlic and season with salt and pepper.

3. To make the salsa, combine the remaining cucumber with onions, mint, parsley and ½ tsp lemon juice. Season with salt and pepper.

4. In a saucepan, heat oil and sauté garlic with oregano and rosemary. Season with salt and pepper. Add chicken and cook.

5. Using the prepared garlic oil, brush one side of the bread and broil it for about 3 minutes or until it looks golden brown.

6. Spread tsatsiki on the bread and serve it with the chicken.

42

Eggplant Frittata

4 servings

This lovely dish is a perfect addition to your breakfast or brunch spread. It is simple but heavily loaded with flavors. You will surely be delighted with every bite.

Ingredients

- 2 ounces Gruyere cheese, grated
- 8 eggs
- ½ pound eggplant, peeled and cubed
- 6 garlic cloves, crushed
- 2 tbsp olive oil
- 1 onion, chopped
- 1 tbsp parsley, chopped
- salt and pepper, to taste

Instructions

1. Season eggplant with salt. Set aside for an hour, then rinse dry with paper towels.
2. In a skillet, heat oil and sauté the onion. Add the garlic and eggplant. Reduce to medium heat and cook the eggplant until it is golden.
3. In a bowl, combine the cheese with egg. Season with salt and pepper.
4. Bring the egg mixture to the pan with the eggplant and pour it in. Make sure to spread it so that it covers the entire skillet.
5. Sprinkle with parsley on top.

43

Gnocchi with Zucchini Ribbons and Parsley Brown Butter

4 servings

This dish is lovely, especially if you are fond of potatoes. Gnocchi is a special Italian favorite and while this makes use of store-bought potatoes, know that you can make gnocchi on your own.

Ingredients

- 2 tbsp butter
- ½ cup parmesan cheese, grated
- 1 pound gnocchi
- ¼ tsp nutmeg, grated
- ½ cup parsley, chopped
- 2 shallots, chopped
- 1 pint cherry tomatoes, halved
- 1 pound zucchini, thinly sliced
- salt and pepper, to taste

Instructions

1. In a saucepan, boil water and cook the gnocchi. You will know they are cooked when they start to float.
2. In a skillet, heat the butter and do so until it starts to brown.
3. Add the zucchini and shallots, then cook until the vegetables are tender.

4. Add tomatoes, nutmeg, salt and pepper. Stir everything together and let the tomatoes break. Then add the parsley and the parmesan cheese.

5. Add the gnocchi and make sure that everything gets coated well.

44

Feta and Marinated Nicoise Olives with Grilled Pitas

8 servings

Ingredients

- 2 bay leaves
- 8-12 pita bread
- 1 pound feta cheese
- 1 garlic clove, sliced
- Japanese or English cucumber spears
- 1 lemon
- 1 cup Nicoise olives
- 2 tbsp olive oil
- 1/3 cup extra-virgin olive oil
- 6-inch rosemary sprig, chopped
- 2 to 3–inch thyme sprigs, chopped
- black pepper to taste

Instructions

1. In a bowl, combine 4 strips of lemon zest, garlic, rosemary, thyme, bay leaves pepper, extra-virgin olive oil and olives. Mix well and let the olives marinate for about 2 hours, up to a month.
2. Prepare the grill.
3. Get pita bread, brush it with oil. Season it with salt and pepper. Grill pita for about a minute per side.
4. On a platter, add the feta cheese and the marinated olives. Serve it with grilled pita and cucumber spears on the side.

45

Spanakorizo

4 servings

This is an amazing twist to the famous spanakopita. Spanakorizo makes use of an interesting mix of ingredients and makes a perfect side dish or vegetable entrée. It features spinach, creatively combined with rice for a perfect medley.

Ingredients

- 2 tbsp dill
- ½ lemon, juiced
- 1 tsp mint
- 2 ½ tbsp olive oil, plus extra
- 1 onion, chopped
- 1 pound spinach
- 1/3 cup brown rice
- 1 tbsp tomato paste (optional)
- 2/3 cups water
- salt and pepper, to taste

Instructions

1. In a pot, combine the lemon juice, 1 tsp olive oil and spinach. Cook until the spinach has wilted. Drain and set aside.
2. In another pot, heat the remaining oil and sauté the onions until they are tender. Add the spinach.
3. Add the water, mint and dill. Let it boil.
4. Add rice. Season with salt and pepper. Let everything simmer. Feel free to add more water if necessary.

46

Crispy Chicken Stew with Lemon, Artichokes, Capers and Olives

4 servings

What a party in your mouth this dish will be. The name itself sounds so fun so just imagine how it is when you actually taste it. This is a good meal to have with the family. It will surely bring a smile to everyone's faces.

Ingredients

- 2 cups artichoke hearts
- 3 cups chicken broth
- ¼ cup capers with brine
- 2 pounds bone-in chicken thighs
- 2 garlic cloves, minced
- 1 tbsp granulated garlic
- 2 tbsp ghee (or olive oil)
- ½ lemon, thinly sliced
- 1 cup kalimata olives
- ½ red onion, chopped
- 1 tsp dried oregano
- 1 ½ tsp fresh oregano, chopped
- 1 tsp sea salt
- ¼ cup white wine

Instructions

1. In a bowl, bring together granulated garlic, dried oregano and ½ tsp sea salt.
2. Add the chicken and rub the seasoning all over. Making sure to coat all sides evenly. Set it aside. (You may marinate up to 24 hours).
3. In a skillet, heat ghee or oil and sauté the marinated chicken. Then remove it from skillet and pat it dry with paper towels. When dry, take it back to the skillet and fry it with the skin down, this time. Cook until brown.
4. Using the same skillet, add capers, garlic, onions and the rest of the sea salt.
5. Add the lemon slices and stir occasionally.
6. Add the white wine to deglaze the skillet and let it simmer.
7. Add the broth and the chicken mixture and let everything simmer for about 5 minutes.
8. Add the artichoke hearts with the olives and let it simmer.
9. Take the chicken out and roughly chop it, discarding the bones. Bring back the meat to the skillet and make sure to coat it well with the sauce.
10. Serve with a garnish of fresh oregano.

47

Baked Falafel

2 servings

Put in some work on this lovely vegetarian patties delight and feast on the mixture of flavors. The spices mix perfectly together and create a great experience for your senses.

Ingredients

- ¼ tsp baking soda
- 1 egg, beaten
- ¼ tsp ground coriander
- 1 tsp ground cumin
- 1 tbsp all purpose flour
- 15 ounce garbanzo beans, rinsed and drained
- 3 cloves garlic, minced
- 2 tsp olive oil
- ¼ cup onion, chopped
- ¼ cup parsley, chopped
- ¼ tsp salt
- cheesecloth

Instructions

1. Preheat oven to 400°F.
2. Using a cheesecloth, wrap the onion and squeeze it to remove the moisture, and set it aside.
3. In a food processor, put in the parsley, garlic, garbanzo beans, cumin, baking soda and coriander. Let it run until it is pureed coarsely. Transfer it to a bowl.

4. Add egg and flour into the bowl. Toss in the dried onions and knead them together. Form patties (about four) and let it set for about 15 minutes.
5. In a skillet, heat oil and cook the patties until it is golden brown.
6. Pop the skillet into the oven and bake it for about 10 minutes.

48

Courgette and Quinoa-Stuffed Peppers

4 servings

Who said great food needs to be complicated. This dish brings together 5 different ingredients to create such a simple, yet amazing dish. It will definitely be a hit on the dinner table.

Ingredients

- 85g feta cheese, crumbled
- 1 courgette, sliced
- 1 handful parsley, chopped
- 4 red peppers
- 2 (250g) packs of quinoa

Instructions

1. Preheat oven to 400°F.
2. Take the peppers and cut them in half. Remove the seeds and stems. Lay them on a baking sheet and drizzle it generously with olive oil. Pop them into the oven until they have softened a little.
3. In a pan, heat oil and cook the courgettes until they have softened.
4. Transfer to a bowl and add the quinoa, parsley and feta cheese. Season with salt and pepper, to taste.
5. Scoop the quinoa mixture into the peppers and bring them back into the oven. Let everything cook for about 5 minutes.

49

Garlicky Greek Salad

6 servings

This dish showcases such simplicity in the bowl but brings true excitement on the palate. It is very simple to prepare and is ideal for a busy day. Prepare the dressing ahead of time and toss it in with your veggies when you're ready.

Ingredients

- ¾ cup feta cheese, crumbled
- 1 tbsp garlic, chopped
- 2 tbsp lemon juice
- 1 head red leaf lettuce, coarsely chopped
- ½ cup olives, pitted and coarsely chopped
- 6 tbsp olive oil
- 3 roma tomatoes, seeded and coarsely chopped
- 1 tsp red wine vinegar

Instructions

1. In a bowl, combine the olive oil, lemon juice, garlic and red wine vinegar. Let it set for about 3 hours.

2. In a salad bowl, combine the tomatoes, lettuce, olives and cucumber. Whisk the dressing and pour into the bowl. Toss the salad and make sure to coat everything evenly.

3. Serve with feta cheese on top.

50

Grilled Chicken, Red Onion and Mint Kebabs

4 servings

There are days when you deserve something indulgent and if this is one of those days, then you have the right recipe to tackle. The flavors of oregano and mint go very well together, in a wonderful surprise.

Ingredients

- 4 cloves garlic, crushed
- 1 ½ pounds chicken breast fillet, sliced
- 2 tbsp lemon juice
- 1 tsp dried mint
- 1 bunch fresh mint
- 4 tbsp extra-virgin olive oil
- 1 red onion, sliced
- 1 tsp oregano
- salt and black pepper, to taste
- 8 metal skewers

Instructions

1. In a bowl, combine chicken with 2 tbsp oil, mint, garlic, oregano, salt and pepper. Let the chicken marinate for about 30 minutes.

2. In a small bowl, use the remaining oil and mix it with lemon juice.

3. Prepare the grill.

4. Skewer the chicken. Alternate it with onion and mint leaves. Season with salt and pepper. Grill until chicken is cooked. Baste it occasionally with the oil and lemon marinade.

5. Serve with salad, pita or rice.

51

Chorizo Pilaf

4 servings

This is a Mediterranean twist to the Spanish paella and Italian risotto. It is an amazing and flavorful rice dish that allows your senses to travel with every spoonful.

Ingredients

- 2 bay leaves
- 250g chorizo, sliced
- 4 garlic cloves, crushed
- ½ lemon, zest peeled in strips
- ½ lemon, wedges
- 1 tbsp olive oil
- 1 onion, sliced
- 1 bunch parsley, chopped
- 1 tsp smoked paprika
- 250g basmati rice
- 600ml stock
- 400g can chopped tomato

Instructions

1. In a pan, heat oil and sauté onion until it is tender.
2. Add the chorizo and cook it until it is browned.
3. Add the paprika and garlic. Add the tomatoes and let it cook until it forms bubbles on the surface.

4. Add the stock, rice, bay leaves and lemon zest. Mix everything together and let it boil. Cover it and let it simmer.

5. Serve with parsley and lemon wedges.

52

Ravioli and Vegetable Soup

4 servings

You may think this is a light soup dish, but the ravioli changes the game and will surely give you a satisfying fill. The flavors are interesting and you will surely delight at the taste it offers.

Ingredients

- 1 tsp basil or marjoram
- 1 cup bell pepper, diced
- 15 ounces vegetable or chicken broth
- 2 cloves garlic, minced
- 1 tbsp extra-virgin olive oil
- 1 cup onions, diced
- 6 to 9 ounces whole wheat ravioli pasta
- 28 ounces canned tomatoes, crushed
- 1 ½ cups hot water
- 2 cups zucchini, diced
- ¼ tsp red pepper, crushed (optional)
- pepper, to taste

Instructions

1. In a saucepan, heat oil and sauté onion, garlic, bell peppers as well as the crushed peppers if you are using some. Stir everything together for about a minute.
2. Add the broth, basil or marjoram, water and let everything come to a boil.
3. Add the ravioli and let it cook accordingly.
4. Add the zucchini and cook it until it is tender and crisp.
5. Season with pepper to taste.

53

Greek Burger with Arugula, Tomatoes and Feta

4 servings

How about some burgers today? This is a delicious burger recipe that's so exciting with every bite. The patty is incredibly moist and flavorful. Instead of bread, this is paired with whole-wheat pitas.

Ingredients

- 3 cups arugula
- 1/3 cup feta cheese, crumbled
- 2 cloves garlic
- ¾ pound lean ground lamb
- 1 tbsp lemon juice
- 2 tsp olive oil
- 1 onion, finely chopped
- 1 red onion, sliced
- 4 tsp oregano, chopped
- ¼ cup skim milk
- 2 tbsp mint, fresh
- 4 whole wheat pitas
- 1 tomato, sliced

Dressing:

- ½ cup cucumber, peeled, seeded and finely diced
- 2 tsp garlic, chopped
- 1 tsp honey
- 1 tbsp mint, chopped

- ➤ 2 tsp Dijon mustard
- ➤ 2/3 cup plain yogurt

Instructions

1. Preheat oven to 350°F.
2. On each pita, cut about ¼ from it and chop them coarsely, and soak it in milk. Drain and squeeze excess milk from pita bread.
3. In a food processor, blend soaked pita, garlic, onion, mint, oregano and lemon juice.
4. Get the lamb. Season with salt and pepper. Combine with the pita sauce, then form patties.
5. In a skillet, heat oil and cook the burgers to medium.
6. In a bowl, mix yogurt, garlic, mint, honey and mustard. Add the cucumber and season it with salt and pepper.
7. Take the pita bread, stuff it with arugula and add some dressing. Lay the burger on it with tomato and red onion on top. Serve with feta and dressing on the side.

54

Caponata

6 servings

Do you fancy a nice Sicilian veggie dish? This fantastic recipe makes good use of aubergines and plays with flavors in such an interesting way. Serve it best with ciabatta bread, or let your creativity fly.

Ingredients

- 3 aubergine, cubed
- 1 handful basil
- 2 tsp capers
- 4 celery sticks, sliced
- 100ml olive oil
- 1 handful pine nuts
- 50g raisins
- 50ml red wine vinegar
- 2 shallots, chopped
- 4 roma tomato, chopped
- salt and pepper, to taste

Instructions

1. In a saucepan, heat oil and add the aubergines. Cook them until they are tender. Remove aubergines and set them aside.

2. On the same pan, add the shallots and cook them until they are transparent.

3. Add the tomatoes and allow them to break. Bring back the aubergines.
4. Add the raisins, capers, vinegar and celery. Season with salt and pepper, to taste.
5. Cover everything and let it simmer in low heat for about 40 minutes or cook it until the vegetables are tender.
6. Serve with ciabatta bread.

55

Greek Mussels and Potato Stew

4 servings

Here is an enjoyable dish that creatively uses mussels. Northern Greeks are very fond of mussels and this stew features their lovely favorite in a very unique and flavorful way.

Ingredients

- 1 carrot, thinly sliced
- 2 garlic cloves, thinly sliced
- 20 mussels, scrubbed and debearded
- ¼ cup olive oil
- 2 onions, chopped
- 3 tbsp parsley, chopped
- 2 russet potatoes, peeled and cubed
- 3 tomatoes, peeled, seeded and diced
- 1 ¼ cups water

Instructions

1. In a saucepan, heat oil and sauté garlic until it's soft.
2. Add tomatoes, potatoes and carrots. Reduce heat and let it simmer until it thickens.
3. Add parsley and water. Cook everything until the potatoes are tender. Season with salt and pepper.
4. Add the mussels and cover. Cook until the mussels open.

56

Mediterranean Quinoa Salad

8 servings

This is a very interesting way to enjoy quinoa. The flavors combine in such an amazing way and the hint of lemon zest just seals the deal.

Ingredients

- 1 tbsp balsamic vinegar
- 1 green bell pepper, diced
- ½ cup feta cheese, crumbled
- ¼ cup chives, chopped
- 2 cubes chicken bouillon
- 2 chicken breast, cooked and diced
- 1 clove garlic, smashed
- ½ cup kalamata olives, chopped
- 2/3 cup lemon juice
- ¼ cup olive oil
- 1 onion, diced
- ¼ cup parsley, chopped
- 1 cup quinoa, uncooked
- ½ tsp salt
- 2 cups water

Instructions

1. In a sauce pan, heat some water and add the cubes with the garlic. Let it boil.
2. Add the quinoa, Reduce the heat and cover. Let it simmer for about 15 to 20 minutes. Remove the garlic and transfer the quinoa to a bowl.
3. Add the feta cheese, chicken, bell pepper, onion, parsley, chives, olives and salt into the bowl.
4. Pour in the balsamic vinegar, olive oil and lemon juice. Toss everything well and make sure to coat all the ingredients with the dressing.

57

Spinach with Chili and Lemon Crumbs

4 servings

This is a very interesting twist to the leafy spinach. It is seasoned to showcase a spicy kick and then served with lemon for perfect texture and boldness of flavour. It will definitely be a memorable dish to have.

Ingredients

- 100g breadcrumbs
- 25g butter
- 1 red chilli, finely chopped
- 1 cloves garlic, crushed
- 500g spinach
- 1 lemon, zest

Instructions

1. In a large pan, melt butter and allow it to foam before you add the breadcrumbs.
2. Add the lemon zest, chilli and garlic. Cook everything until the garlic is golden and the lemon is crunchy. Season with salt and pepper. Set aside.
3. Using the same pan, add the spinach and cook it until it is wilted. Stir it continuously while cooking. Serve it with the crumbs sprinkled on top.

58

Greek Orzo and Shrimp Salad

20 servings

Salad dishes are among the simplest and easiest dishes to make. But contrary to what others think, salads are more than just vegetables. Maybe a piece of vegetable is worth nothing, but when the medley of flavors comes together, it plays a symphony that's too beautiful to resist. This Greek orzo salad is just that—it is amazing how something this simple can taste so good.

Ingredients

- ¾ feta cheese, crumbled
- 1 ½ cucumbers, cubed
- 1 ½ cucumbers, sliced into rounds
- ¾ cup dried dill, chopped
- fresh dill sprigs
- 7 tbsp lemon juice
- 6 tbsp olive oil
- 1 ½ bunch green onions, chopped
- 1 ½ pound orzo pasta
- 3 pounds uncooked shrimp, peeled and deveined
- 2 baskets cherry tomatoes, halved

Instructions

1. Cook orzo pasta accordingly. Drain and place in a large bowl.
2. Add feta cheese, green onions, chopped dill, oil and lemon juice. Mix everything well.
3. In a pot with salt and water, boil the shrimps until they are pink. Drain and rinse. Mix with the salad. Season with salt and pepper.
4. Add the cucumber slices and cherry tomatoes to the salad.
5. Serve with a garnish of dill sprigs.

59

Tortellini Primavera

5 servings

Here's another pasta dish that's going to win your heart. It showcases a selection of lovely vegetables, adding texture, color and taste to the dish. Enjoy it with a whole wheat baguette or savor it on its own.

Ingredients

- 14 ounces vegetable or chicken broth
- 1 cup parmesan cheese, grated
- 2 tbsp all purpose flour
- 3 cloves garlic, sliced
- 1 tbsp extra-virgin olive oil
- 1 tbsp tarragon, chopped (dill or chives)
- 16 ounces whole wheat tortellini pasta
- 4 cups assorted vegetables, chopped (carrots, broccoli, snap peas)
- salt, to taste

Instructions

1. In a large pot, boil some water.
2. In a small bowl, whisk the flour into the broth and mix it well. Set aside.
3. In a skillet, sauté garlic until it starts to brown, then add the broth. Bring everything to a boil.
4. Remove from the heat and add the cheese, salt and tarragon (or dill or chives). Mix it well.

5. Add the tortellini and the assorted vegetables to the boiling water set earlier. Let it simmer until they are all cooked. Drain the water and add with it the contents of the skillet. Make sure to coat the tortellini evenly.

60

Greek Chicken Pasta

2 servings

How about some pasta today? You may use any type of pasta you prefer for this dish, but be smart enough to choose whole wheat. This is surprisingly filling without being too heavy and most of all, sinful.

Ingredients

- 14 ounces artichoke hearts, chopped
- 1 pound chicken breast fillet, diced
- ½ cup feta cheese, crumbled
- 2 cloves garlic, crushed
- 2 lemons, wedged
- 2 tbsp lemon juice
- 1 tbsp olive oil
- ½ cup red onion, chopped
- 2 tsp oregano
- 16 ounces whole wheat pasta
- 3 tbsp parsley, chopped
- 1 tomato, chopped
- salt and pepper, to taste

Instructions

1. Cook the pasta accordingly. Set aside.
2. In a skillet, heat oil and sauté garlic and onion until fragrant.
3. Add the chicken and cook until it is no longer pink.

4. Add the tomatoes, artichoke hearts, parsley, feta cheese, oregano, lemon juice and the cooked pasta. Heat everything for about 3 minutes and remove it from the heat.

5. Season with salt and pepper. Garnish with lemon wedges and serve.

61

Mussels with Tomatoes and Chili

2 servings

If you love seafood and you adore spicy food, then you will definitely love this dish. It is an adventurous seafood dish that plays with magnificent flavors.

Ingredients

- 1 handful basil
- 1 red or green chilli, seeded and finely chopped
- 1 clove garlic, finely chopped
- 1kg mussels, cleaned
- 2 tbsp olive oil
- 1 shallot, finely chopped
- 1 pinch sugar
- 2 tomatoes
- 1 tsp tomato paste
- 1 glass dry white wine

Instructions

1. In a bowl, pour boiling water over the tomatoes and let it blanch. Drain the water. Seed the tomatoes and roughly chop it. Set aside.
2. In a pan, heat oil and sauté the garlic, chilli and shallot until tender.
3. Add the wine, tomato paste, sugar and tomatoes. Season with salt and pepper.
4. Add the mussels into the pan and cover it. Cook it until the mussels have opened. Remove the pieces that did not open.
5. Serve with basil, on top.

62

Greek Chicken and Vegetable Ragout

6 servings

This is a lovely chicken dish with a very interesting Greek sauce that showcases that freshness of lemon zest. Chicken is light and the breast portion is the healthiest, but at the same time it is filling.

Ingredients

- 15 ounces artichoke hearts, quartered
- 14 ounces chicken broth
- 1 pound carrots, chunks
- 2 pounds chicken, shredded
- 1/3 cup dill, chopped
- 1 egg
- 2 egg yolks
- 4 cloves garlic, minced
- 1/3 cup lemon juice
- 1 pound potatoes, wedges
- 1/3 cup white wine
- salt and pepper, to taste

Instructions

1. In a slow cooker pot, lay the potatoes and carrots at the bottom.
2. Put the chicken on top of the vegetables.
3. In a saucepan, combine the broth, garlic, wine and salt. Bring it to boil over medium heat. Pour this mixture

over the chicken and vegetables. Leave it on the slow cooker for about 3-4 hours.

4. Once cooked, add the artichokes and cooker for about 5 minutes.
5. In another bowl, mix the whole egg, egg yolks and lemon juice together.
6. Take about ½ a cup of the cooking broth and mix it with the eggs. Whisk everything well until you achieve a smooth consistency.
7. Remove the chicken and vegetables from the cooker and lay them on your serving bowl.
8. Take the egg mixture and pour the entire contents into the slow cooker. Whisk until it is thick. Pour it on the chicken and vegetables and serve.

63

Tuscan-Style Tuna Salad

4 servings

The best thing about whipping up a salad is that it requires very little fuss. You do not have to cook it; you just have to mix it well. As long as the flavors are properly mixed and the choice of vegetables is great, the dish becomes satisfying. This recipe can also be used to make fillings for wraps and sandwiches, so feel free to transform it to a more filling meal.

Ingredients

- 15 ounces white beans or cannelini
- 2 tbsp lemon juice
- 2 tbsp extra-virgin olive oil
- 4 scallions, trimmed and sliced
- 10 cherry tomatoes, quartered
- 6 ounces tuna chunks, drained
- salt and pepper, to taste

Instructions

1. In a bowl, mix all the ingredients together.
2. Refrigerate for a few hours before serving.

64

Chicken Kofte with Zucchini

4 servings

This is a great chicken dish that is very simple, yet definitely flavorful. The ingredients blend well to create a party of different flavors in your mouth.

Ingredients

- ¼ cup breadcrumbs
- 1 pound ground chicken
- 1 tsp ground cumin
- 5 tbsp mint, chopped
- 4 tsp olive oil, divided
- ¼ cup onion, grated
- 1/8 tsp ground red pepper
- ½ cup tzatziki, divided
- 4 zucchini, halved
- salt and pepper, to taste

Instructions

1. Preheat broiler to high.
2. In a bowl, mix the ¼ cup tzatziki, onion, breadcrumbs, cumin, 3 tbsp mint and red pepper. Season with salt and pepper.
3. Add the ground chicken and mix everything together. Do not be afraid to use your hands. Create 8 patties.
4. In a skillet, heat oil and cook the patties until they are golden brown.

5. Get a broiling pan and grease it. Lay the zucchini on top and season it with salt and pepper. Pop it into the broiler and cook until it is tender.

6. Serve the kofte with zucchini. Add the remaining tzatziki on the side.

65

Spinach and Feta Pita Bake

6 servings

This is an interesting way to enjoy spinach. It is a light dish or a pretty appetizer that comes with a surprising crunch, just when you finish off your bite.

Ingredients

- ½ cup feta cheese, crumbled
- 2 tbsp parmesan cheese, grated
- 4 mushrooms, sliced
- 3 tbsp olive oil
- 6 whole wheat pita breads
- 1 bunch spinach, chopped
- 2 roma tomatoes, chopped
- 6 ounces sundried tomato pesto sauce
- salt and black pepper, to taste

Instructions

1. Preheat oven to 350°F.
2. Lay the pita bread open on a baking sheet and spread tomato pesto sauce over on one side. Layer each pita bread with tomatoes, mushrooms, spinach, parmesan cheese and feta cheese.
3. On the very top, drizzle with olive oil. Season it with salt and pepper.
4. Pop the baking sheet into the oven and bake everything until the pita bread is crisp.

66

Baked Parmesan Tomatoes

4 servings

This simple recipe is a good one for snack time. Stay away from the unhealthy choices and switch to something that is good for your body. These baked tomatoes are truly exciting and they are quite easy to make.

Ingredients

- ¼ cup parmesan cheese, grated
- 4 tsp extra-virgin olive oil
- 1 tsp oregano, chopped
- 4 tomatoes, halved
- salt and pepper, to taste

Instructions

1. Preheat oven to 450°F.
2. On a baking sheet, lay the tomatoes and top it with oregano, parmesan cheese, salt and pepper.
3. Drizzle with oil and pop it into the oven. Let it bake until the tomatoes become tender.

67

Chicken Souvlaki

4 servings

This is a simple take on the classic souvlaki. It may be eaten as a snack, with your hand. But you can also choose to lay it on your plate and eat it daintily with a knife and fork.

Ingredients

- 1 1/3 pound chicken breast fillets, cubed
- 6 tbsp butter
- 1 cucumber, peeled, seed and grated
- ¼ tsp dill
- 1 clove garlic, minced
- 1 ½ tsp lemon juice
- 1/3 cup kalamata olives, halved and pitted
- 2 tbsp olive oil
- 1 onion, sliced
- 1 tbsp oregano
- 4 pita bread
- 2 tomatoes, sliced
- 2 cups yogurt
- salt and pepper, to taste

Instructions

1. Strain the yogurt and let it drain in the refrigerator.
2. In a bowl, combine cucumber and salt to remove its liquid. Add the yogurt to the cucumber. Add garlic, dill and pepper.

3. Preheat the broiler.

4. In a stainless steel bowl, mix the oregano, lemon juice and oil. Season with salt and pepper. Add the chicken cubes and make sure to coat the meat evenly.

5. Arrange the chicken on the skewers and grill the chicken. Set aside.

6. Take the pita bread and butter both sides. Lay them on the broiler until it is golden, then cut them into quarters.

7. Arrange everything on the plate. Lay the pita with the chicken skewers and serve it with tomatoes, olives and onions on the side.

68

Spice Sweet Roasted Red Pepper Hummus

8 servings

Hummus is a staple in Mediterranean diets and this is an interesting hummus recipe that is a little step away from its traditional taste, with a kick of spice that truly adds some character to the dish.

Ingredients

- ½ tsp cayenne pepper
- ½ tsp ground cumin
- 15 ounces garbanzo beans
- 1 clove garlic, minced
- 3 tbsp lemon juice
- 1 tbsp parsley, chopped
- 4 ounces roasted red peppers
- ¼ tsp salt
- 1 ½ tbsp tahini

Instructions

1. Pop in all the ingredients into a food processor and blend everything well until you achieve a smooth and fluffy texture.
2. Refrigerate it for about an hour before serving.
3. Garnish it with parsley on top.

69

Paprika Shrimp and Green Bean Sauté

6 servings

This is a lovely garlicky shrimp dish with a lovely kick. Cook the green beans with a crisp for an amazing texture and serve this with quinoa if you wish to add more substance. Otherwise this is good on its own.

Ingredients

- 16 ounces butter beans or cannellini
- 4 cups green beans, trimmed
- ¼ cup garlic, minced
- 3 tbsp extra-virgin olive oil
- 2 tsp paprika
- ½ cup parsley, chopped (divided)
- 1 pound raw shrimp, peeled and deveined
- ¼ cup sherry vinegar
- salt and pepper, to taste

Instructions

1. In a saucepan, let the green beans steam until it is tender-crisp. Cover it.
2. In a skillet, heat oil and sauté garlic and paprika, until fragrant.
3. Add the shrimps until it has a lovely pink color.
4. Add the beans, salt and vinegar. Mix everything well, then add the parsley.
5. Lay the green beans on the serving plate and top it with the shrimp mixture.
6. Season with pepper and garnish with parsley.

70

Artichoke and Arugula Pizza with Prosciutto

4 servings

This is the go-to recipe if you want to splurge and celebrate a little. This amazing dish is sincerely intense with its characteristic addictive flavour. Everyone says that pizza is love... this one is going to be worth it.

Ingredients

- 9 ounces artichoke hearts, coarsely chopped
- 1 ½ cups arugula
- 1 ½ tbsp lemon juice
- 2 tbsp mozzarella cheese
- 2 tbsp parmesan cheese
- 1 tbsp cornmeal
- 13.8 pizza crust dough
- 2 tbsp prepared pesto sauce
- 1 ounce prosciutto

Instructions

1. Preheat oven to 500°F.
2. Grease the baking sheet and sprinkle it with cornmeal.
3. Take the dough and lay it on the baking sheet. Spread the pesto sauce and sprinkle mozzarella cheese on the surface. Make sure to cover the entire surface evenly. Pop it into the oven and cook for about 5 minutes.

4. Take the pizza out and lay the artichokes on top. Add prosciutto and sprinkle it with parmesan cheese. Bring the pizza back to the oven and let it cook for about 6 minutes.

5. Take the pizza out and top it with arugula. Slice the pizza and serve.

71

Bean Bolognese

4 servings

This is a fiber-rich bean pasta dish that's uniquely satisfying. It is unlike any other vegetarian pasta you've had before. Pair it with bread or a light salad—but feel free to have it on its own.

Ingredients

- 1 bay leaf
- 14 ounces salad beans, divided
- ½ cup carrot, chopped
- ¼ cup celery, chopped
- ½ cup parmesan cheese, grated
- 2 tbsp extra-virgin olive oil
- 4 cloves garlic, chopped
- 1 onion, chopped
- 8 ounces whole wheat fettuccine
- 14 cup parsley, chopped
- 14 ounces canned tomatoes, diced
- ½ cup white wine
- salt, to taste

Instructions

1. Cook pasta accordingly. Set aside.
2. In a small bowl, mash ½ cup of beans. Set aside.
3. In a saucepan, heat oil and sauté onions.

4. Add the celery, carrot and salt. Then cook covered until the vegetables are tender.
5. Add the garlic and bay leaf. Stir continuously until fragrant.
6. Add wine and increase the heat. Cook until wine reduces.
7. Add the tomatoes, mashed beans and parsley.

72

Greek and Penne Chicken

4 servings

If you fancy some pasta today, here is a very simple pasta dish that's quite light, so you do not have to worry about packing some extra calories. The flavors are quite simple but they combine very well together.

Ingredients

- 14 ounce artichoke hearts
- 1 ½ tbsp butter
- 1 pound chicken breast fillet, diced
- ½ cup feta cheese, crumbled
- 2 cloves garlic, minced
- 2 tbsp lemon juice
- ½ cup red onion, chopped
- 1 tsp oregano
- 3 tbsp parsley, chopped
- 16 ounces whole wheat penne pasta
- 1 tomato, chopped
- ground black pepper, to taste

Instructions

1. Cook pasta accordingly. Set aside.
2. In a large skillet, heat oil and sauté garlic and onion until fragrant.
3. Add chicken and cook it until it is golden brown.

4. Add the artichoke hearts, feta cheese, chopped tomatoes, lemon juice, parsley and oregano in. Reduce the heat.

5. Add the pasta and stir together. Make sure you mix everything well. Season with salt and pepper.

73

Catalan Sautéed Polenta and Butter Beans

4 servings

Let this amazing dish take you to Spain with every bite. It is a lovely vegetable dish that boasts very interesting flavors.

Ingredients

- 15 ounces butter beans, rinsed
- 1 red bell pepper, diced
- ¾ cup vegetable broth
- ½ cup Manchego or Monterey Jack cheese
- 1 clove garlic, minced
- 4 tsp extra-virgin olive oil, divided
- 1 onion, halved and sliced
- ½ tsp paprika, smoked (plus for garnish)
- 16 ounces polenta, cubed
- 4 cups baby spinach
- 2 tsp sherry vinegar

Instructions

1. In a skillet, heat 2 tsp oil and cook the polenta until they begin to brown. Set aside.
2. Using the same pan, heat the remaining oil and sauté garlic until fragrant then add onions and bell pepper. Sauté until tender and sprinkle it with paprika. Stir constantly.

3. Add the beans, broth and spinach. Stir constantly and cook until spinach is wilted. Remove from heat.
4. Add the cheese and vinegar. Mix everything together.
5. Serve this mixture over the polenta and garnish it with paprika.

74

Seared Mediterranean Tuna Steaks

4 servings

If you love fish, this is a great recipe that brings out the true character of tuna. The unique lemon-sage flavour is going to be amazing, and will surely complement with the fish. Enjoy this with a side of salad or potatoes.

Ingredients

- 1 tbsp capers
- ½ tsp ground coriander
- ½ tsp garlic, minced
- 1 tbsp lemon juice
- 12 kalamata olives, chopped
- 1 tbsp extra-virgin olive oil
- ¼ cup green onions
- 3 tbsp parsley, chopped
- 1 ½ cups tomato, seeded and chopped
- 4 yellow fin tuna steaks
- salt and pepper, to taste

Instructions

1. Sprinkle it with salt and pepper. Add the coriander.
2. In a skillet, add oil and fry the fish, cooking both sides well.
3. In a bowl, mix together the tomatoes with the rest of the ingredients to create the salsa. Season this with salt and pepper. Serve it on top of the fish.

75

Mustard-Crusted Salmon

4 servings

This is a very interesting salmon recipe. It may not appeal to you right away but it is going to amaze you and your palate.

Ingredients

- lemon wedges
- 2 tsp lemon juice
- 2 tbsp stone ground mustard
- 1 ¼ pounds salmon fillets
- ¼ cup sour cream
- salt and pepper, to taste

Instructions

1. Preheat broiler.
2. Get a broiler pan or baking sheet and line it with foil. Coat the same with cooking spray.
3. Lay the salmon fillets, skin down, and season with salt and pepper.
4. In a bowl, mix the sour cream, lemon juice and mustard. Spread this mixture over the salmon.
5. Pop the salmon in the broiler and cook until the center is cooked.
6. Serve with lemon wedges on the side.

76

Greek Style Potatoes

4 servings

This is such a creative way to enjoy potatoes. Add a bit more of lemon if you fancy more zest, or enjoy it simply and allow the ingredients to party in your mouth with their different flavors.

Ingredients

- 2 cubes chicken bouillon
- 2 cloves garlic, finely chopped
- ¼ cup lemon juice
- 1/3 cup olive oil
- 6 potatoes, peeled and quartered
- 1 tsp rosemary
- 1 tsp thyme
- 1 ½ cups water
- ground black pepper, to taste

Instructions

1. Preheat oven to 350°F.
2. In a bowl, combine the oil, garlic, lemon juice, water, thyme, chicken bouillon, rosemary and pepper together. Set aside.
3. On a baking dish, arrange the potatoes evenly and lay the mixed ingredients on top of the potatoes, making sure to cover everything well.
4. Cover the dish with foil and pop it in the oven. Bake until the potatoes are tender.

77

Rigatoni with Green Olive-Almond Pesto and Asiago Cheese

6 servings

If you like pesto, this is a very unique take on the classic dish. Instead of the usual ingredients, the pesto sauce is made from olives and almonds. This gives the dish a very characteristic flavor that you won't forget.

Ingredients

- ½ cup asiago cheese, grated
- ½ cup almonds, sliced and toasted
- 1 clove garlic, minced
- 1 ¼ cups manzanilla olives (or green olives)
- 1 pound rigatoni pasta
- ½ cup parsley
- 2 tbsp water
- 1 tsp white vinegar
- pepper, to taste

Instructions

1. Cook pasta accordingly. Set aside.
2. In a food processor, blend the olives, almonds, garlic, parsley and pepper. Blend until it is coarsely chopped.
3. Add water and 1 tsp vinegar into the pesto mixture. Blend it again until everything is finely chopped.
4. Combine the pesto sauce with the pasta. Toss it well to make sure that the rigatoni is evenly coated.
5. Sprinkle cheese on top and serve it.

78

Sausage, Mushroom and Spinach Lasagna

10 servings

Here's an indulgent dish to enjoy. It is perfect for entertaining a few people. You can feast on something tasty, without it being sinful. Make sure to use whole wheat lasagna, but feel free to substitute the Italian sausage with a vegetarian alternative.

Ingredients

- ¼ cup basil, chopped
- 8 ounces mozzarella cheese, shredded (divided)
- 1 pound ricotta cheese
- 4 cups mushrooms, sliced
- 8 ounces whole wheat lasagna
- 1 pound lean spicy Italian sausage (or vegetarian sausage)
- 1 pound spinach
- 28 ounces canned tomatoes, crushed
- ¼ cup water
- salt and pepper, to taste

Instructions

1. Preheat oven at 350°F. Prepare a baking dish and coat with cooking spray.
2. Cook pasta accordingly. Set aside.
3. Coat a skillet with cooking spray and cook the sausage until it has crumbled.
4. Add mushrooms and water. Stir it constantly until the mushrooms are tender and the sausage is completely crumbled.
5. Add the spinach, but squeeze it to release excess water before doing so.
6. In a bowl, combine the basil with salt and pepper.
7. Arrange the lasagna on the baking dish. Making sure to have well spread layers of filling and pasta. Start with a layer of tomato filling then a layer of pasta. Add ricotta cheese then spread a thick layer of sausage mixture over it. Add tomatoes, mozzarella, and cover it with a layer of pasta. Repeat the previous layering technique then after you cover the dish with pasta, simply finish it with the extra tomatoes.
8. Cover the dish with foil and let it bake for about 1 hour or until it begins to bubble. Once cooked, take it out and sprinkle a layer of mozzarella, then pop it back into the oven and let the cheese melt.

79

Greek Tzatziki

40 servings

If you fancy snacking and you would love a good dip to use for your vegetable sticks, you can create this tzatziki. You do not have to be guilty about snacking with this vegetable dip. The yield for this recipe is quite large so you can have this for awhile. Just store it properly in bottles and keep it in the refrigerator.

Ingredients

- ½ cucumber, peeled and grated
- 3 tbsp dill, chopped
- 1 clove garlic, pressed
- 2 tsp lemon zest, grated
- 2 tbsp lemon juice
- 2 tbsp extra virgin olive oil
- 32 ounce plain yogurt
- salt and pepper, to taste

Instructions

1. In a bowl, combine the cucumber, yogurt, lemon juice, garlic and olive oil together.
2. Add dill, pepper, salt and lemon zest. Mix thoroughly until you achieve a smooth paste.
3. Store in bottles and refrigerate for about 8 hours before serving.

80

Garlic-Rosemary Lamb Pita

4 servings

Sometimes you deserve a pat on the back and this lamb recipe will surely do that very well. The savory strips of meat are flavoured generously. It will let your taste buds travel.

Ingredients

- 1 ½ cups cucumber, finely chopped
- 1 tsp garlic, minced
- 1 tbsp lemon juice
- 1 pound boneless leg of lamb, cubed
- 2 tsp olive oil
- 4 pitas
- 1 tbsp rosemary, chopped
- 6 ounces yogurt
- salt and pepper, to taste

Instructions

1. In a bowl, mix the lamb, garlic and rosemary. Season it with salt and pepper. Set aside.
2. In a skillet, heat oil and sauté the lamb mixture until the meat is properly cooked.
3. In a bowl, mix the cucumber, yogurt and lemon juice. Season it with salt and pepper.
4. Arrange the pitas. Divide the lamb mixture. Add the yogurt mixture and serve.

81

Easy Arugula Salad

4 servings

How about a salad dish that's easy to make? Salads are the least complicated meals that you can toss together. This arugula salad is simple, but absolutely enjoyable. You have the option to alternate between olive oil and grapeseed oil, depending on availability or preference.

Ingredients

- 4 cups young arugula
- 1 avocado, peeled, pitted and sliced
- ¼ cup parmesan cheese, grated
- ¼ cup olive oil (or grapeseed oil)
- ¼ cup pine nuts
- 1 cup cherry tomatoes
- 1 tbsp vinegar
- salt and pepper, to taste

Instructions

1. In a large bowl, combine all the ingredients together, except for the avocado slices. Mix well and if you have a bowl with lid, use it so you can cover it and shake the contents to mix things evenly.
2. Serve it with avocado slices for garnish.

82

Smoky Corn and Black Bean Pizza

6 servings

This is a very beautiful grilled pizza dish that's heavenly packed with flavour and nutrients. Its colors will be definitely satisfying and the taste will perfectly seal the deal, so brace for something amazing.

Ingredients

- 1/3 cup barbecue sauce
- 1 cup black beans
- 1 cup corn kernels
- 2 tbsp cornmeal
- 1 cup mozzarella
- 1 pound prepared whole wheat pizza dough
- 1 roma tomato, diced

Instructions

1. Preheat grill to medium.
2. In a bowl, bring together the tomatoes, corn and beans.
3. On a baking sheet, sprinkle cornmeal and lay the pizza dough on top.
4. Grill the dough for about 4 to 5 minutes or until the crust is light brown.
5. Flip the crust and assemble the pizza on the grilled side. Start with the barbecue sauce. Add the tomatoes and bean mixture, then add the cheese.
6. Cover the grill and let the pizza cook until the bottom is brown.

83

Greek-Style Scampi

4 servings

Scampi is ordinarily cooked by submerging the shrimps in butter. But for the healthy alternative, this Mediterranean take makes use of olive oil. It showcases the same interesting flavors and gives it a unique and unforgettable twist.

Ingredients

- ¾ cup feta cheese, crumbled
- 4 cloves garlic, minced
- 1 ½ tbsp lemon juice
- 1 tbsp olive oil
- ¼ cup parsley, chopped and divided
- 1 ¼ pounds shrimps, peeled and deveined
- 14 ½ ounces whole peeled tomatoes, chopped
- salt and pepper, to taste

Instructions

1. Preheat oven to 400°F.
2. Using a Dutch oven, heat oil and sauté garlic. Cook until slightly browned.
3. Add the tomatoes and parsley. Season it with salt. Reduce the heat and let everything simmer.
4. Add the shrimps and sprinkle it with feta cheese.
5. Pop it into the oven for about 10 minutes.
6. Top it with parsley and lemon juice. Season it with salt and pepper.

84

Pasta Fagioli Soup

8 servings

Sometimes there are days when you just want a nice bowl of soup and if today is that day, then this very tasty Italian soup is going to be perfect. It is rich in flavor and is a little indulgent with the use of bacon. Discard it from the ingredients if you wish it out, but a little portion is not going to be bad.

Ingredients

- 8 slices cooked bacon, crumbled
- ½ tsp basil
- 14 ounces beans
- 14 ounces chicken broth
- 1 tbsp garlic, minced
- 1 tsp garlic powder
- ½ pound seashell pasta
- 1 tbsp parsley
- 14 ounces spinach, chopped
- 8 ounces tomato sauce
- 29 ounces canned tomatoes, diced
- 3 cups water
- salt and pepper, to taste
- parmesan cheese (optional)

Instructions

1. In a deep pot, put together the beans, tomatoes, tomato sauce, spinach, garlic, chicken broth, garlic, garlic powder, parsley, bacon, basil, water, salt and pepper. Let it boil. Cover it then leave it simmering for about an hour.
2. Add the pasta, stirring occasionally and cook until pasta is al dente.
3. Serve with a sprinkle of parmesan cheese on top.

85

Italian Egg-Drop Soup

6 servings

To transform the traditional dish into a meal, some adjustments have been made to the original. For instance, pasta was added, as well as arugula and chickpeas. This gave the simple egg-drop soup more substance, so it is definitely more filling.

Ingredients

- 3 cups arugula, chopped
- 6 tbsp parmesan cheese
- 6 cups chicken broth
- 7 ounces chickpeas, rinsed
- 4 eggs, lightly beaten
- 2 tbsp lemon juice
- 1 pinch of nutmeg
- 1 1/3 cups whole wheat pasta shells
- 1 bunch scallions, sliced (greens and whites divided)
- 2 cups water
- pepper, to taste

Instructions

1. In a Dutch oven, bring together the pasta, scallion whites, chickpeas, water, broth and nutmeg. Cover and bring to a boil. Uncover and let it simmer for about 4 minutes.
2. Add arugula and let it cook until it is wilted.

3. While stirring, add the eggs slowly. Season with salt and pepper.
4. Add the lemon juice and scallion greens.
5. Serve with a sprinkle of parmesan cheese, on top.

86

Greek-Flavored Turkey Burgers

4 servings

What better way to enjoy lean meat, but in a burger? This burger recipe introduces an interesting surprise with every bite: the unique crunch of red onions, the burst of feta cheese and the lingering flavour of mint. Serve this with a side of vegetables or enjoy it on its own.

Ingredients

- 7 ounces roasted red bell peppers, sliced
- ½ cup breadcrumbs
- 4 whole wheat buns
- 1/3 cup feta cheese, crumbled
- 1 tsp dill
- 1 egg white
- ¾ cup mint, chopped
- 2 tbsp lemon juice
- 1 cup red onion
- 1 pound ground turkey

Instructions

1. In a bowl, beat the egg whites and add the onions to the mixture.
2. Add the mint, breadcrumbs, feta cheese, lemon juice, dill and ground turkey. Make sure to mix everything well. Use your hands if you must. Form patties.

3. In a skillet, apply grease and cook the patties on both sides.

4. To serve, arrange the patties with the bun, with the top half laid open. Serve the peppers on top of each.

87

Avocado and Tuna Tapas

4 servings

Tapas is a staple in Spain and here is a nice healthy version of the famous tapas. Feel free to substitute the vegetables with those you prefer. Experiment with color, texture and taste.

Ingredients

- 2 ripe avocados, halved and pitted
- 1 dash balsamic vinegar
- ½ red bell pepper, chopped
- 3 green onions, thinly sliced
- 1 tbsp mayonnaise
- 12 ounces tuna in water, drained
- salt and pepper, to taste

Instructions

1. In a bowl, combine the mayonnaise, tuna, red bell pepper, green onions and balsamic vinegar. Reserve a few green onions for garnish.
2. Season it with salt and pepper.
3. Get the halved and pitted avocados and serve the tuna salad into the halves.
4. Garnish with green onions and serve.

88

Corn and Broccoli Calzones

6 servings

Here is an interesting way to enjoy whole wheat dough—turn it into calzones. A calzone is a folded pizza, so it looks more like a pie. This healthy calzone is absolutely delicious and you can serve it with a light marinara sauce, to add an interesting kick to it.

Ingredients

- ¼ cup basil, chopped
- 1 ½ cups broccoli florets, chopped
- 1 cup mozzarella cheese, shredded
- 2/3 cup ricotta cheese
- 2 tsp canola oil
- 20 ounces prepared whole wheat pizza dough
- ½ tsp garlic powder
- all purpose flour (for dusting)
- 1½ cups corn kernels
- salt and pepper, to taste

Instructions

1. Preheat over to 475°F.
2. In a bowl, bring together the corn, broccoli, ricotta, mozzarella, scallions, garlic powder, basil, salt and pepper.
3. Spread flour on the table and prepare the dough for the calzones. Scoop a generous amount of filling into each

of the dough then fold it to close it. Crimp the edges with a fork to seal it, but don't forget to create small slits on the center to function as vents.

4. Lay the calzones on the baking sheet. Pop the baking sheet into the oven and let it cook until it has browned.

89

Saffron Fish Stew with White Beans

4 servings

If not for the richness in color alone, saffron truly has the capacity to transform a dish into something special. This fish stew recipe boasts the blend of different herbs and spices to present a wonderful phenomenon on the diner table.

Ingredients

- 14 ounces great northern beans
- 1 ½ cups clam juice
- ½ tsp coriander
- 1 tsp ground fennel
- 1 pound flounder fillet, cubed
- 2 cloves garlic, crushed
- 1 tbsp extra-virgin olive oil
- 1 cup onion, chopped
- ½ tsp orange rind, grated
- ¼ tsp. saffron threads, crushed
- 1 thyme sprig
- 1 bunch fresh thyme
- 14.5 ounces canned tomatoes, diced
- 1 ½ cups water
- salt, to taste

Instructions

1. In a Dutch oven, heat oil and sauté the fennel, onion, coriander and thyme sprig.

2. Add the orange rind and saffron.
3. Add water, tomatoes and clam juice. Bring everything to boil and reduce heat. Let it simmer for about 5 minutes.
4. Add the fish and beans. Season with salt and cook everything for about 5 minutes.
5. Serve with a dash of thyme leaves.

90

Slow Cooker Mediterranean Stew

10 servings

Here is a stew recipe, fit for a feast. If you are entertaining some friends and you are looking for a winner dish that is perfect for entertaining, this is what you need. The flavors are definitely interesting and it is built to please. Most especially, it is healthy.

Ingredients

- ½ cup vegetable broth
- 1 carrot, julienned
- ¼ tsp ground cinnamon
- ½ tsp ground cumin
- 2 cups eggplant, cubed
- 1 clove garlic, chopped
- 10 ounces okra, thawed
- 1 cup onion, chopped
- ¼ tsp paprika
- ¼ tsp red pepper, crushed
- 1/3 cup raisins
- 1 butternut squash, peeled, seeded and cubed
- 1 tomato, chopped
- 8 ounces tomato sauce
- ½ tsp turmeric
- 2 cups zucchini

Instructions

1. In a slow cooker, pop in all of the ingredients together. Mix well.
2. Cover and let everything cook for about eight to ten hours. The vegetables should be nice and tender.

91

Lemony Asparagus Pasta

2 servings

This is a fresh pasta dish with a lovely hint of lemon. Cook it well, and the asparagus will give your bite a very interesting crunch. Savor the creaminess of the sauce and inhale all the flavors.

Ingredients

- ½ bunch asparagus, trimmed and cut
- ½ cup parmesan cheese, grated and divided
- 2 tbsp garlic, minced
- 1 tsp extra-virgin olive oil
- 2 tsp all purpose flour
- 1 tsp lemon juice
- ¾ cup whole milk
- 2 tsp whole grain mustard
- 4 ounces whole wheat penne pasta
- 1 tsp tarragon, minced
- salt and pepper, to taste

Instructions

1. Cook the pasta accordingly and add the asparagus. Stir constantly until the pasta is cooked right. Drain and set aside.

2. In a bowl, combine the milk, flour, mustard, flour, salt and pepper. Set aside.

3. In a saucepan, heat oil and sauté garlic until fragrant.

4. Add the milk mixture and let it simmer.
5. Add the tarragon, lemon juice and lemon zest.
6. Add the cooked pasta and continue to stir everything until the sauce thickens. Let the sauce coat the pasta evenly.
7. Serve it topped with parmesan cheese.

92

Halibut with Lemon-Fennel Salad

4 servings

This uniquely season fish dish is not a traditional find, but it is a welcome experience for every type of diner. The tangy taste of lemon gives it a characteristic freshness that allows your senses to travel.

Ingredients

- 1 tsp ground coriander
- ½ tsp ground cumin
- 2 cups fennel bulbs, thinly sliced
- 2 cloves garlic, minced
- 4 halibut fillets
- 2 tbsp lemon juice
- 5 tsp extra-virgin olive oil, divided
- ¼ cup red onion, thinly sliced
- 1 tbsp parsley
- 1 tsp thyme
- salt and pepper, to taste

Instructions

1. In a bowl, mix coriander, salt, cumin and pepper.
2. Combine 1 ½ tsp of this spice mixture with 2 tsp oil and garlic.
3. Get the fish and rub it generously with the garlic and spice sauce.

4. In a skillet, heat oil and cook the fish. Make sure to cook it properly.
5. In another bowl, mix the remaining spice mixture with 2 tsp oil, fennel and all the remaining ingredients.
6. On a plate, lay the fish and serve the salad beside it.

93

Spanish Cod

6 serving

This is a perfect day for some fish. Seafood is a great source of healthy fats and today is just a day for that. This delicious dish has a tomato base and a medley of different vegetables. The star of this dish is cod fish but to add a seafood component, feel free to blend in a few pieces of jumbo shrimps.

Ingredients

- 1 tbsp butter
- 6 cod fillets
- ½ cup green olives, chopped
- 1 tbsp olive oil
- ¼ cup onion, finely chopped
- 1 dash paprika
- 1 dash cayenne pepper
- 15 cherry tomatoes, halved
- 1 cup tomato sauce
- ¼ cup deli marinated vegetables, coarsely chopped
- 2-3 pieces of jumbo shrimps (optional)
- salt and pepper, to taste

Instructions

1. In a large skillet, heat the butter and sauté the garlic and onions, until tender.
2. Add the cherry tomatoes and tomato sauce. Let things simmer.

3. Add the green olives, cayenne pepper, paprika, marinated vegetables, salt and pepper.
4. Add the cod fillets and cook until they easily flake.
5. Add the prawns with shells, if you are going to use some prawns.
6. Serve immediately. This is good to enjoy while it is hot.

94

Easy Salmon Cakes

4 servings

Omega-3 is good fat and it is found in most fishes. Fat often scares a lot of people but omega-3 is rich in fat that you can trust. This simple salmon cakes recipe is a fun way to enjoy fish.

Ingredients

- 1 ¾ whole wheat bread crumbs
- 1 stalk celery, diced
- 1 large egg, lightly beaten
- 1 lemon, wedges
- 3 tsp extra-virgin olive oil
- 1 onion, finely chopped
- 1 ½ tsp Dijon mustard
- 2 tbsp parsley, chopped
- 15 ounces salmon
- pepper, to taste

Instructions

1. Preheat oven at 450°F.
2. Get a baking sheet and coat it generously with cooking spray.
3. In a skillet, heat ½ tsp oil and sauté onions. Add the celery and cook until they are tender.

4. In a bowl, break the salmon in flakes and discard the skin. Add mustard and egg and mix everything well together.

5. Add the onion mixture, pepper and breadcrumbs. Blend it well and form 8 patties.

6. In the same skillet, heat the remaining oil and cook the patties until they are golden brown.

7. Finally, pop the fried patties into the oven and let them bake for about 15 to 20 minutes. Serve with lemon wedges and a cream sauce.

95

Mediterranean Chicken with Eggplant

5 servings

This is a simple traditional Mediterranean recipe that is rich in heavenly flavors. It is the type of dish that a mother passes along to her daughter and goes down the line.

Ingredients

- 6 chicken breast fillets, diced
- 3 eggplants, peeled and cut lengthwise
- 3 tbsp olive oil
- 1 onion, diced
- 2 tsp oregano
- 2 tbsp tomato paste
- ½ cup water
- salt and pepper, to taste

Instructions

1. Preheat the oven to 400°F.
2. In a large pot, lay the strips of eggplant at the bottom and cover it with water. Season it with salt and let everything soak for about 30 minutes until the water is salty and brown.
3. Take the eggplants out and brush each of them with olive oil.
4. Sauté in a pan or grill on a baking dish. Set the eggplants aside.

5. In a skillet, heat oil and sauté the onions until tender and add the chicken.

6. Add the tomato paste and water then cover everything to allow it to simmer.

7. In a baking dish, lay the eggplants and pour the tomato and chicken mixture over it. Season with oregano, salt and pepper. Cover the dish with foil and pop it in the oven. Let it bake for 20 minutes.

96

Turkey Kefta Patties with Cucumber Salad

4 servings

If you are having a nice barbecue on a hot summer day, this lovely burger recipe is surely going to be the star of the show. The unique burst of flavor will not disappoint and surely, all your guests will go home with a great memory of this dish.

Ingredients

- ¼ cup cilantro, chopped
- ½ tsp ground cinnamon
- 2 tsp ground coriander
- 2 cups cucumber, sliced
- 1 tsp ground cumin
- 1 tbsp ginger, peeled and chopped
- 1 tbsp lemon juice
- ¼ cup parsley, chopped
- 2 pitas
- 1 pound ground turkey
- 2 tbsp rice vinegar
- ½ cup yogurt
- salt and pepper, to taste

Instructions

1. Preheat grill pan at medium heat. Grease it.
2. In a bowl, mix the ground turkey, cilantro, ¼ cup parsley, ginger, coriander, cumin, salt and cinnamon.

Make sure to blend everything well and use your hands if necessary. Shape the mixture into patties.

3. Cook the patties on the grill pan and do so until it is properly cook.
4. In another bowl, mix the cucumber and vinegar together.
5. In yet another bowl, mix the yogurt with the parsley, lemon juice and pepper.
6. Arrange everything on the plate. Lay the patty and serve the cucumber salad on the side. Add a dollop of the yogurt sauce on top. Finally, place the pita wedges on the plate.

97

Tabouleh

4 servings

Bulgur is a cereal food that comes from wheat. This is a common ingredient in Mediterranean dishes and it is the star in the popular Tabouleh. This is a unique type of salad dish that is flavorful and truly enjoyable.

Ingredients

- 1 cup bulgur
- 1 cucumber, peeled, seeded and chopped
- 1/3 cup lemon juice
- ¼ cup mint, chopped
- 1/3 cup olive oil
- 1 cup green onions, chopped
- 1 cup parsley, chopped
- 3 tomatoes, chopped
- 1 2/3 cup boiling water
- salt and pepper, to taste

Instructions

1. In a large bowl, combine the bulgur and the boiling water. Cover it and let it set for about an hour.
2. After an hour, add all the other ingredients into the bowl. Season it with salt and pepper to taste. Cover it and refrigerate it for about an hour before serving.

98

Sweet Sausage Marsala

6 servings

How about a very unique pasta dish that uses Marsala wine? The flavor of the sausage and the richness of the wine bring an interesting experience to your mouth.

Ingredients

- 1 green bell pepper, sliced
- 1 red bell pepper, sliced
- 1 clove garlic, minced
- ½ onion, sliced
- 1 pinch oregano
- 16 ounces bowtie whole wheat pasta
- 1 pound mild Italian sausage
- 14.5 ounces canned tomatoes, diced
- 1/3 cup water
- 1 tbsp Marsala wine
- salt and black pepper, to taste

Instructions

1. Cook pasta accordingly. Set aside.
2. In a skillet, heat 1/3 cup water and cook the sausages. Cover it until it is cooked. Drain and slice thinly.
3. In a skillet, heat the sausage. Add the onions, garlic, wine and bell peppers. Cover it and reduce the heat.
4. Add the diced tomatoes, oregano and pepper.
5. Combine with pasta and serve.

99

Crisp Lamb Lettuce Wraps

4 servings

This is a very light dish that you can eat with pita, hummus or flatbread. You can have it as a snack or a perfectly healthy light dish.

Ingredients

- 1 tsp ground cinnamon
- ½ cup cucumber, chopped
- 2 tsp garlic, minced
- ¼ cup red pepper hummus
- 6 ounces ground lamb
- 8 lettuce leaves
- 2 tbsp mint leaves, torn
- 1 onion, finely chopped
- 2 tsp olive oil
- ½ cup parsley, chopped
- 1 tbsp pine nuts, toasted
- ½ cup tomato, chopped
- ¼ cup yogurt
- salt and pepper, to taste

Instructions

1. In a skillet, heat oil and sauté onion.
2. Add the lamb and let it cook until it is done. Set aside.
3. In a bowl, mix the parsley, cucumber and tomato. Add the lamb and onion mixture.

4. In yet another bowl, mix the yogurt and the hummus.
5. On a plate, lay the lettuce leaf and top it with lamb. Add a dollop of the hummus and yogurt mixture on top.
6. Finally sprinkle it with mint and pine nuts.

100

Spicy Sage and Olive Hash Brown

2 servings

For breakfast, here is a unique hash brown recipe that is definitely flavorful and fun.

Ingredients

- 1 cup black olives, sliced
- 2 tbsp olive oil
- 4 ounces onion, chopped
- ¼ cup parsley, chopped
- ¼ tsp crushed red pepper flakes
- 3 cups frozen hash brown potatoes
- 2 tbsp sage, minced
- salt, to taste

Instructions

1. In a bowl, mix together the olives, onions and potatoes. Add the sage, red pepper flakes and 2 tbsp of parsley. Season it with salt. Set it aside.
2. In a skillet, heat oil and fry the hash browns until they are golden and crispy.
3. Sprinkle with parsley on top.

Conclusion

In Conclusion, I would like to thank you once again for taking action by purchasing this book. I hope this book shall help you achieve your wellbeing objectives. Wishing you all the best and good luck!

Printed in Great Britain
by Amazon